HAVING
IT
BOTH
WAYS

Also by Elaine Denholtz

PLAYS

Frozen
The Dungmen Are Coming
Hey Out There, Is There Anyone Out There?
Some Men Are Good at That
An Even Exchange
The Highchairs
Love Games

FILMS

Summerhill
Waiting . . . The Life Styles of the Elderly
The Dental Auxiliary
What's Inside
Is That What You Want for Yourself?
Another Mother (Eugene O'Neill adaptation for television)

BOOKS

Education, Where It's Been, Where It's At, Where It's Going
  (contributor)
The Highchairs
How to Save Your Teeth and Your Money (co-author)
The Dental Facelift (co-author)

HAVING IT BOTH WAYS

a report on
Married Women with Lovers

ELAINE DENHOLTZ

STEIN AND DAY/*Publishers*/New York

First published in 1981
Copyright © 1981 by Elaine Denholtz
All rights reserved
Designed by Louis A. Ditizio
Printed in the United States of America
STEIN AND DAY/*Publishers*
Scarborough House
Briarcliff Manor, N.Y. 10510

Library of Congress Cataloging in Publication Data

Denholtz, Elaine.
  Having it both ways.

Bibliography: p.
  Includes index.
  1. Adultery. 2. Married women. I. Title.
HQ806.D46   306.7'3   81-40336
ISBN 0-8128-2819-4   AACR2

To Mel
and
To my mother, Lillian Sachs Grudin,
who told me that the best stories are love stories

Acknowledgments

You've probably watched it on television. The Oscar Awards. The tension is high, the envelope is torn open, and the name is triumphantly announced. The winner then strides to the microphone to make the acceptance speech—a stream of *thank yous*, naming all the people who contributed to the film's success. In this way, the movie world makes public acknowledgments.

No such high drama accompanies the publication of a book. Even books that win awards are not celebrated with hoopla and television cameras. Generally, the author simply places an acknowledgment page at the beginning of the book. Few bother to read it.

Perhaps this is due to the myth that an author is a solitary creature who toils alone, perhaps for years, with only the *click-clack* of the typewriter for company. True? Not entirely.

This book took over three years. But I did not do it alone. So many people cheered me on. Although the writing was done alone in the little office my husband built for me behind the garage (some walk-in closets are larger), the mulling over, the conceptualization, the sounding off were often done with people whose opinions I valued and whose judgments I trusted. Everyone who talked to me—psychologists, social workers, physicians, authors, therapists, psychiatrists, teachers, counselors, colleagues, family, and friends—made a special contribution to this book. I bounced ideas off them. I examined their thoughts. And I came to focus this book more clearly because of the conversations we had. They were my allies. In that sense, no book is written alone.

To Maria Carvainis, my agent, goes the lion's share of my gratitude. She believed in this project from the start and never wavered in her determination to place the manuscript with a good publisher. She also supported and encouraged me along the way with just the right words when I needed them. Her intelligence and genuine feel for the material made a sizable contribution to this book.

To Jill Neimark, I am grateful for her considerable editorial comments and her fastidious attention to detail. Her respect for words helped me clarify many points.

To Benton Arnovitz, my editor, I am in debt for his thoughtful suggestions, his keen eye, and his good judgments. His skillful editing helped me make this book more readable.

To Sol Stein and Pat Day, my publishers, I am grateful for their enthusiastic response to the project, for their experienced and valuable criticisms, and for their excellent suggestions. Their practical advice helped me shape the tone of the book.

I am also grateful to Barbara Solomon, who typed the interviews from the original tapes. Sometimes she listened to a passage over and over to make sure she got it exactly right, every word, laugh, and sigh.

To my husband, my father, and my children, this book must have seemed a real enemy, usurping my time and my thoughts for so long. But they understood. Often, they tip-toed around me, pitched in to run off Xerox pages, and dashed to the post office for me. Most of all, they let me know they cared about how the work was going. They were with me all the way.

But the ineffable debt is to all the women who talked to me, who took time out of their busy lives to set the record straight. The heart of this book is the words of these women. They gave me the gift of their stories. Without them, there would be no book. So this book is their book, too.

Many confirmed what I felt from the start: the need for a book about married women with lovers. Because almost nothing had been written on the subject which allowed women to speak for themselves, most welcomed the chance to share their experiences.

In opening their homes and their hearts to me, they had to go back and review their lives. Had to reveal powerful emotions. Had to churn up old wounds. Had to reexamine relationships with their parents, children, husbands, and lovers. This often meant experiencing those pains and triumphs all over again. It wasn't easy. These women had courage. To tape-record the events of an ongoing or past affair can be scary. It's a risk. These women were brave, open, and sincere. In allowing me to probe tender spots, they had to expose intimate, private details. They had to come to terms with their motivations, options, and choices. They had to relive secret moments. This must have cost them something.

Because I pledged them anonymity, I cannot name them. However, they made the truest contribution to this book. Indeed, they are this book. When they read their interviews, I hope they will feel proud that they were part of this project. I hope they will nod approval and take pleasure in the job I've done. Although their contributions cannot be publicly acknowledged, and no Oscars or television cameras will honor them, they know who they are. To every one of them, I gratefully offer my thanks and my affection.

CONTENTS

Preface

The women in this book are real; they are not composite or fictional characters. However, I have deliberately assigned them fictitious names, occupations, and geographic locations, and have altered other details to protect their privacy. But the words they speak are their words—taped and edited for publication. These are true stories, and I am tremendously indebted to these married women with lovers for sharing the intimate details and emotions of their personal experiences.

Elaine Denholtz

INTRODUCTION

One out of three married women has a lover.*

Next time you're standing in a line—at the bank, at the movies, in any public place—try counting heads. One, two, *three*. One, two, *three*. Some of the women may be standing next to their husbands, but a third of them are or were in someone else's bed this week or last week or some time not too long ago.

Up to now, it was only men who kissed and told. Until recently, a married woman who had an affair kept it secret. Hid it from even her closest friends. Was torn up inside. Felt torment, indecision, guilt—and most of all, felt alone.

For husbands, it was different. From biblical times history has recorded their affairs, and usually their infidelity is accepted with no more than a *tch-tch*, a slap on the wrist. Although privately a man's wife may be deeply wounded, public reproach is rare. Husbands can have affairs, even flaunt them openly.

* "Redbook Report on Female Sexuality," 1978.

Having It Both Ways

But wives? No.

Yet every wife has wondered what it would be like to sleep with another man. To have a secret lover. To know romance, intrigue, passion. So if you've ever wondered about having an affair, you're not alone. If you've ever considered meeting an attractive man after work, getting involved in an extramarital relationship, these women's stories will inform you about the pleasures and agonies of it. If you've ever thought about another man, even though you care for your husband, what these women have to say will speak to you.

While wives rarely brag about it, they are doing it. Sometimes with guilt and at great cost. Sometimes with sheer pleasure. Some are even saying they are entitled to the same code of values that men are: the respectability of marriage, and the pleasures of an extramarital affair.

An affair, at the start, can be like going to a movie. Something intrigues you. You step into the theater. The lights go down and almost effortlessly you're caught up in an experience full of gratification, pleasure, and relief from daily conflicts.

It may seem tremendously exciting at first, because it's new and different. But if your affair begins to take on the signs of real romantic love—heartache, frequent thoughts of your lover wherever he is, pain at his absence, ecstatic anticipation of your next meeting—you are suddenly on an out-of-control roller coaster ride in which you will laugh and cry—sometimes in the same instant— and you may not know how to stop, how to get off, to say, "Enough!"

Yet many women who take a lover find themselves bursting out of a fifteen- or twenty-year cocoon. They often reexperience "falling in love" with all the first intensity of their youth. They may even feel that they have only now discovered what love really means.

Despite today's predilections for surveys, questionnaires, and reports, the statistics tell only the driest story. The percentages tell us little about women's feelings or those of their husbands, lovers, and children. One learns quickly that a 200-page questionnaire is not twice as valid as a 100-page questionnaire.

Before I began this book I tried to answer a number of the

pollsters' queries myself and found that I couldn't answer them comfortably. Here, for example, is one that stumped me— Question 59 from "The Redbook Report on Female Sexuality":

Of all aspects of sexual activity, which one do you like best?

31.1%	A.	Everything
19.6	B.	Intercourse (Hite,* are you listening?)
23.1	C.	Orgasm
16.9	D.	Foreplay
3.6	E.	Masturbation (Barbach,† are you listening?)
10.2	F.	Oral sex
0.7	G.	Anal sex
20.8	H.	Satisfying my partner
40.3	I.	Feeling of closeness with my partner

Wouldn't you have trouble with this one? I noted that sexual fantasies (Friday,‡ are you listening?) were absent from the list. So were sadomasochism, pornography, incest, dressing up, and homosexuality. Women were allowed to give multiple answers, so the percentages were the most mystifying of all.

In some cases, my honest response to a question was "yes *and* no." Or my answer fell midway between "rarely" and "sometimes." How do you fit that on a graph? I was convinced the interview would be more responsive to feelings than surveys and statistics.

Interviews with real women in genuine life situations would serve as the spine of the book's authority. I spoke with over one hundred women, and selected ten featured interviews to represent the most powerful and recurring motivations women have expressed for their affairs. The additional vignettes throughout the book further illustrate these motivations. Here are some of the questions I asked; they are merely starting points for the stories that came pouring out:

1. How did you meet your lover?
2. What does he look like?

* Shere Hite, author of *The Hite Report, Sexual Honesty* and *The Hite Report on Male Sexuality.*
† Lonnie Garfield Barbach, author of *For Yourself.*
‡ Nancy Friday, author of *My Secret Garden.*

3. What do you like about your husband?
4. What are the risks in taking a lover?
5. What were your motivations?
6. What made you choose *him* for a lover?
7. What is your relationship to your husband? Your parents? Your children?
8. How do you perceive your own emotional needs?
9. How do you manage your love affair?
10. Where do you meet your lover? How often?
11. Do you always have sex?
12. What does the affair cost you?
13. How do you hide it?
14. How long has it been going on?
15. How would your husband and kids feel if they found out?
16. What turns you on or off sexually?
17. How is your lover different from your husband?
18. Would you want to marry your lover?
19. How has your affair affected your marriage?
20. Is sex the most important aspect of your affair?
21. If you had to do it over, what would you change? Any regrets?
22. *Can* married women have it both ways?

This book took focus when I realized I was hearing one particular theme quite regularly: Wives who took lovers felt *they were entitled to it*. Although women in the past were beset with guilt, these women felt they were not doomed to settle for an unsatisfactory marriage. They felt they deserved more than they were getting—deserved love and happiness. They felt they had good reasons to seek out another partner.

This book does not make a case for wives to take lovers. It is neither polemic nor prophetic. Yet knowledge can be gained from the stories of women who have had an affair—have chosen lovers as an alternative: women who, like men for centuries before them, no longer accept the exclusivity code in marriage. Women who have acknowledged their appetites, their needs, dreams, and longings, and who have taken charge of their lives. Women who seek pleasure and intimacy with another man, and above all, women who are honest and open enough to tell their stories in this book.

HAVING
IT
BOTH
WAYS

1

A Little Band
of Gold

"HAVE YOU NOTICED," she asked, "that being a married woman doesn't seem to turn men off anymore? They still come on to us."

I was talking with a young woman—probably rounding thirty—whom I'd just met at a noisy party. We were chatting easily, moving from one subject to another: our work, our families, our frustrations. Since there was more than a decade of summers between us, I was amused and flattered that she grouped us together: two married women who turn men's heads and hearts. Although the line of impatient lovers had not yet formed at my front door, I was eager to hear more.

"What do you mean," I asked, "that men still approach us?"

"*You* know," she said. "The fact that a woman wears a wedding ring doesn't mean a thing anymore. Right?"

I returned only a soft *mmmmm*, and my silence drew her out.

"I mean ten years ago when I was single," she continued, "a married woman was out of bounds. Once she flashed her ring, the man got the message."

"And today?"

'Married women are fair game. In fact, being married or single seems as significant as your social security number." She laughed. "He may even know your husband and like him. It doesn't bother him one way or the other."

"What do you think that means?"

"Well . . . maybe there are a lot more married women having relationships outside marriage than we assume."

"You really think so?"

"Sure,"·she said. "One out of four according to Kinsey, and that was back in 1953."

"But look," I protested, "there have always been wives who took lovers. That's not news. Maybe we're just more open about it today. We talk about it more."

"Sure, that's part of it, too," she agreed. "But it's probably a lot more widespread than we commonly acknowledge. Listen," she confided, "two of my friends, married six years and eight years, have lovers. That knocks me out! They're not Emma Bovary. They *care* about their husbands. They don't want to dissolve the marriage, but they have lovers, too. You think that's possible?"

"What?"

"To have an ongoing relationship with a husband and a lover at the same time? To have it both ways?"

That's when this book was born.

Now, under the guise of simple curiosity, I considered the relationships I knew: my own married friends, the women in my family, the women I worked with at the university. To uncover some answers, indeed to couch some intelligent questions, I read widely among the researchers, the social historians, the feminists, the anti-feminists, the sexologists, the psychologists, the psychiatrists, the therapists, and the popular magazine journalists.

What did I uncover?

That the intimate relationships of married men and their lovers have been exhaustively documented. In plays and songs, in histories and biographies, they spilled from the pages. One has only to stand at a supermarket check-out and glance at a magazine to learn of Ike's lover or Elvis' lover or JFK's lover. Everywhere, everyone acknowledges that married men have lovers.

However, with the rare exception of special women like Ingrid Bergman or George Sand, the subject of married women with lovers has been discreetly hidden. This despite hard evidence from Kinsey (who told us more than a quarter of a century ago that one in four wives have affairs by age 40), Masters and Johnson, and Hite.

In 1975, *Redbook* readers answering the magazine's poll updated that information, informing us that the percentage had swelled to 29%. Clearly, an important sociological phenomenon is occurring. And it is outrageously absent from the literature.

Married women with lovers. Why has so little been written on the subject? If nearly one out of three women sprouted hair on their chests or developed an interest in tropical fish, some sociologists, biologists, sexologists, journalists, and psychologists would be tracking down the facts. Why is this subject kept quietly under wraps? And what does it mean when a wife takes a lover? That wives have become increasingly unhappy? Wasn't marriage an all-and-forever contract? Is guilt over adultery now out the window? Are women's expectations in marriage rising so alarmingly that husbands can no longer meet them?

Almost everyone has ascribed motivations for married women taking lovers. After years of living with the same man, a woman may not feel she is getting enough to satisfy her basic needs—enough intimacy, excitement, attention, loving, sex. She may be bored, or disappointed, or terrified of growing old and losing her sexual appeal. If her husband has affairs or is preoccupied with his work, she may feel angry or question her own self. Why doesn't he spend more time with her? For the woman who straddles the responsibilities of career and family, there is often little time to communicate clearly with the man she has chosen to live with. After ten years or more, husband and wife may feel like strangers in their own bed. And, as the years pass, a woman can mature and evolve into someone very different from the "girl" who went straight from her mother's home to her husband's at age 18 or 20. She may, indeed, see herself as an entirely different person. If her husband doesn't respond to that new "self," but another man does, she may find herself rushing headlong into a love affair.

But what about the consequences of that decision? What are the costs? How does it *feel* to have a lover? Does it transform a woman's life? These are questions that can only be answered by the protagonist in this drama: the wife who takes a lover.

Will she say, as one woman did, "It was never like that before, and it never will be again. Yes, it was worth it. It was the most overwhelming experience I have ever had."

Or will she say, as another woman told me, "I felt belittled and diminished by the hiding, the lying. I care for my husband and my children, and I just didn't have enough left over to give my lover. And even though I hurt him by ending it, I knew it was the right decision in the long run."

Who is the married woman who takes a lover?

The first woman I interviewed agreed to have her session with me recorded on tape. I assigned her a code name. We talked for hours. We drank coffee. She broke down and cried. Later, I returned for another interview and we laughed together. She explored, denied, contradicted herself, reassessed, and jumped from one subject to another. She talked about her fears, faced her rage, explained her longings.

"What does it feel like to take a lover?" I asked Betty, a young mother in her twenties who hired babysitters so she could rendezvous with her lover in a distant motel.

Her answer was painful. "I felt lousy," she said.

"How does a working woman manage to have an affair when she's juggling a job, a husband, a house, and kids?" I asked Ada.

Her answer was funny. "Carefully! I'd bring my guy home when my husband and kids were out."

"Where do you find a lover when you're over fifty?" I asked Carol.

Her answer was astonishing. "At fifty you find a *friend* for a lover. I did. Right on my own block," she explained.

"Does it take money to maintain an affair?" I asked Gina.

"You bet it does!" she assured me. "I flew halfway round the world to meet him. The first time in Tel Aviv. And I run whenever he calls. Washington. Paris. New York. And I pay my own way."

Every single interview came out of a personal contact developed at a party, a meeting, almost anywhere. Wherever I mentioned this book, ears perked up and someone knew someone who knew someone who . . . Perhaps because they came by recommendation · through a valued friend, these women felt more at ease. But young or old, married or separated, wives with lovers presently or in the past—each woman felt she had a story to tell, and that the subject of married women with lovers was important.

Betty was in her twenties, Helen was past sixty. Donna is still married, but Ada has divorced. Carol is still with her lover of seven years, but Donna has split from hers. Ellen's first lover was a spiritual man who resisted sex. Fran's lover, 20 years older than she, gave her the best sex she ever had. The varieties and combinations of their motives remain as complex as people are. Only one woman, Irena, was considering a lesbian relationship. The others were all heterosexual.

One woman divorced her husband to marry her lover. Other women left their lovers and stayed with their husbands. Some felt it was impossible, in the end, to have it both ways. Others considered it a fine arrangement.

One wife deliberately took a lover to dissolve her marriage. "It was the one thing he wouldn't stand for," Ada says.

Another wife took a lover to keep the marriage from falling apart. "I would have gone nuts or gotten a divorce if not for my lover. He kept the marriage together and saved my sanity," Fran says.

The women I talked with were basically middle class—not poverty stricken, not millionaires. I learned to avoid the sensationalists and the "spillers." I also excluded promiscuous women, bed-hoppers, and the obviously emotionally ill. A poor welfare wife I tried to interview told me, "Sure I fool around, but I ain't talking to you, lady. My husband would kick my ass in!" A famous international beauty and jet-setter also turned me down, although we had several appointments. She even promised to introduce me to other women, her friends. But each time I phoned, her secretary, her maid, or the children's governess said she was in Cannes or Rome or Paris. *C'est la vie.* Middle-class women were more open and more willing.

Although married women with lovers are a minority—most American women still do not choose to forsake traditional marriage mores—the women you'll listen to here have chosen to have it both ways. As the interviews proceeded, other themes emerged. Certain motifs were repeated. Certain melodies recurred.

Do those melodies and motifs belie the myths we've come to associate with the married woman who takes a lover? I admit that not long ago I believed that old cliché: any wife who has a lover must be locked into an unbearably lousy marriage. I no longer think that is true. You will find that the motivations for these women's extramarital affairs were as varied and complex as human beings are.

In reading their stories, you may even ask yourself, "How different are these women from me?"

The women in this book tell us how they first met their lovers. How the affair caught fire. What lies they told to cover up. Where they rendezvoused. How it felt to have sex with another man. What turned them on or off. How they felt with their husbands. How they kept from being caught. What they did if they were caught.

Have you ever wondered if you could have an affair? Go through with it?

Almost everyone else has wondered, too.

2

Motivations: The Reasons Why They Do It

AS A BRIDE, she swore to love, honor, and cherish 'til death did them part. And she meant it. Her fingers weren't crossed, and her heart was pounding with promise. Then why did she do it? What led her to another man's arms? What turned the romantic bride into the unfaithful wife?

The explanations for infidelity are as varied and contradictory as the people who give them. Adultery is at least as old as the Old Testament. It's probably been with us as long as monogamy has. But it has been strongly condemned and prohibited in most societies. For Jews, the Talmud allowed extramarital intercourse—only if the man accidentally fell off a parapet and consequently landed on top of a woman. (Try that excuse—if you can find a parapet.) While one man–one woman has been viewed as the ideal in the West, many have chosen to look the other way when behavior fell short of the mark. And that was often, perhaps more often than we care to admit.

Americans, particularly, have made the case for fidelity. Perhaps the Puritan background has imposed that unbending code. Americans are more rigid than the English, despite British roots in Victorian behavior. Europeans, with their long history of royal dalliance, illegitimate heirs to the throne, and courtly lovers, take a "civilized" approach to adultery. A European gentleman was not merely *allowed* his liaisons, he was *expected* to keep a mistress. So long as he was discreet, so long as he did not disgrace his wife or dishonor his children, Europeans tended to look the other way.

The nobility were notoriously adulterous. Of Louis XV's mistresses, Madame de Pompadour and Madame du Barry may have been the stars, but the king kept a string of young girls, too. Noble ladies kept their steady lovers as well. Many had two husbands: the one legal spouse and the other their true love. There was no secret about these arrangements, which often lasted ten years or longer. The lady's lover was invited to dinner along with her husband. The English, the French, indeed most of Europe, took this "civilized" approach.

However, even then the double standard was strictly enforced. The Frenchman who enjoyed several mistresses might allow this privilege to his wife, but there were rules to be observed before she could gain his consent. *If* the wife was discreet, *if* her lover was a man of distinction, and *if* she gained her husband's approval first, she might be allowed her lover. But if she didn't secure her husband's permission, he could punish her by locking her up in a convent and garnering her fortune. She, of course, was powerless to punish her husband for the same offense.

This attitude had its roots in the property laws. A wife was a man's property, to be used (or abused) exclusively by him. Furthermore, the double standard had its rationale. The woman's adultery was criminal because it threatened to confuse questions of inheritance. *She* had the baby, so the mother was known. But ascertaining the paternity could prove tricky, and the rightful heirs to property might not be clearly established. Charles II's sexual activities resulted in many bastards. But he was the King.

In America today, the double standard is still alive and well. The man who leads an adulterous life may be envied or admired or excused, but the woman who follows suit is dishonored. Although mistresses, courtesans, and paramours sprinkle the pages of popular journalism, we are still shocked to glimpse our neighbor's wife pulling out of the parking lot of a hotel at midday. We may glance at the headline "I was JFK's Lover" as we stand on the supermarket line, but damn it, it better not happen too close to home! For the working woman, the young mother at home, the average wife in America today, the double standard is still in effect. Infidelity is still socially unacceptable in our personal lives. We may slip from our ideals, but there is no polite and understanding European wink to excuse our behavior.

Rumors about a husband who is keeping a girl friend on the side are often greeted with a clucking of disapproval, a shaking of heads, a sadness of the heart. Still, a man usually escapes serious social consequences.

However, the wife who is fooling around is often ostracized. A "higher" morality is expected from women, especially if the wife is also a mother. The world is still divided into whores and madonnas.

Although sex is a common topic of conversation today, in "mixed company" many take a moral stance. And though ours claims to be a liberated society—permissive to a fault—most people disapprove of infidelity. They call it "cheating," and even the euphemism "fooling around" does not take the sting out of it. Some go so far as to state that adultery committed in the heart is as bad as adultery of the flesh.

Then what motivates wives to take lovers?

Until recently, many psychologists and therapists viewed infidelity as a symptom of emotional disturbance. The extramarital affair was regarded as a sign of a deeply troubled marriage and the adulterer was branded an immature personality. Some counselors labeled infidelity as proof of serious psychological problems that required professional therapy. The unfaithful spouse was said to be acting out an unconscious attempt to force change, or reacting to a deep-seated defense against latent homosexuality.

Other explanations were indictments: The adulterous spouse was unstable, insensitive, selfish and/or cruel. Magazine articles offered opinions by psychologists armed with case histories: Advice columnists told us how to handle the mate who strays. Frequently, these articles took the form of fault-finding, rationalizing, and overinterpreting. Anyone who had an affair could be categorized as either a sickie or a sinner.

These attitudes are slowly evolving, and there is a wider range of acceptance today for varying lifestyles. It is interesting to note that

only since "Gay Power" gained attention have professional attitudes toward homosexuality changed. However, while it is no
longer considered a disease, the stigma of sinning has not been
entirely erased. Homosexuality and infidelity, while adjudged free
of mental disease, are clearly thought by the majority to be less
desirable than a heterosexual preference or married love.

The 1970s saw a change of heart on a number of subjects. Earlier,
psychologist Albert Ellis had argued that there was more to gain
than to lose from infidelity. He cited the need for sexual variety, the
desire for freedom, that marriages can be confining and boring,
that an affair can reduce tension and—hear this—actually improve
a marriage. A flood of defamatory charges was unleashed by his
detractors.

But the novelists, the movie producers, and the television mer-
chants picked up on the theme that adultery could have its benefits.
Soon television audiences could observe book authors, pastors,
actresses, sex therapists—all trying to get their point of view across.
Talk show hosts pitted lively guests against each other, selected
people from the audience to discuss the issues. On the show "Not
for Women Only," the beautiful Christina Paolozzi Bellin, married
to a prominent plastic surgeon, disclosed to Barbara Walters that
she had "a successful husband, two wonderful children and a
fantastic lover."* Adulterers confessed on television, bringing their
tales of infidelity into millions of American homes. "I've had two
long-term affairs in the twenty years I've been married and I can
truthfully say they saved me from a disastrous divorce," a woman
writes to newspaper columnist Helen Bottel. "My current lover is
the greatest. He has helped me understand my husband, showing
that his coldness was partly my fault. You see, he's our minister."
The letter writer concludes with this statement: "I hope this proves
that affairs aren't always hurtful if you're discreet.†

Indeed, media hype notwithstanding, there appears to be some
evidence that an affair may not only give relief to an unhappy

---

* *New York* magazine, June 26, 1978.
† Newark Star Ledger, September 13, 1978.

spouse, but also restructure a stagnant marriage. Some mid-life couples claim their infidelity renewed their marriage and strengthened their bonds. Perhaps no one made the case for this more strongly than the O'Neills, the husband-wife team who wrote *Open Marriage,* a book that extolled the benefits of infidelity. Yet it is interesting to note that Nena O'Neill's later book *The Marriage Premise* did a virtual about-face. The new book endorses sexual exclusivity and the need for loyalty, fidelity, and trust in marriage. So the pendulum swings.

To let you come to know each of these women more easily, their interviews are divided into chapters focused on the motivations of each. These stories stress the human and the intimate. Perhaps it doesn't take years of digging on the psychiatrist's couch to sort it all out. The answer to Freud's eternal riddle, What is it that women truly want? may be found in these women's stories. Surely every husband, wife, and lover is seeking that answer.

And here is something that surprised me. None of the women in this book were overcome by a fit of passion. It did not happen like, as the French expression has it, *un coup de foudre:* no thunderbolt struck. They were not swept off their feet the way the paperback romances like to tell it. They had their reasons, yes. But they weighed it all out. They considered their options. They examined their needs. They led with their heads, not just with their hearts.

"Why did you do it?" I asked every one of these women.

"I was lonely, so lonely," a computer analyst told me. "I just wanted someone to hold me and talk to me."

"I did it to get even. My husband was cheating on me for years," a waitress said.

"Sex with my husband was never very good. I wanted to know what I'd been missing all those years," said a publicity director.

"Why? I fell in love," an actress replied.

So many reasons why wives take lovers. So many reasons why

people fall in love. What are the changing needs a woman experiences which motivate her to reach outside the marriage?

Let's see what these women reveal.

3

COMMUNICATION:
ELLEN AND DONNA

MY TIRES CRACKLED over the white pebbled circular driveway.
Flanked by rhododendrons, azaleas, and hollies, the majestic house
was nestled on five rolling acres in Connecticut in a lovely autumn
setting of orange-tipped oaks and maples. The blue edge of a
swimming pool could be glimpsed across the manicured back
lawn.

Ellen opened the carved entrance door, a slender woman with a
flawless complexion. Green eyes, light brown wispy hair, a simple
but elegant shirtdress. She greeted me with a warm, sweet smile.
She looked in her mid-40s—a good ten years younger than her
actual age. Though not showy, she was obviously a woman of
means. There were no furrows across her forehead. But her mouth
and eyes—they had known pain.

Still, there was a serenity about her and her beautifully decorated
Country French home. The den we sat in was wall-to-wall books.
She brought out a brass tray of coffee and cheeses and crackers.
She had a lovely voice, softly melodic.

"I was born in Brooklyn, yes Brooklyn, and I got married at 19.
When I met Richard, I was 35, married 16 years. I was very excited
by the things he spoke of, his mind, his attitudes about life. He was a
beautiful person, very intelligent. He was 26, single, and of all

things, he was working as a waiter at the country club we belonged to.

"My husband was also a wonderful person. He was a good father—we had a son and a daughter—and he was generous and loving. But I always knew he was not exciting to me intellectually. He wasn't verbal. He wasn't articulate. And he didn't communicate well. Just a sweet, good, hard-working guy. But because he didn't excite me mentally, he couldn't excite me physically. The relationship was pleasant and sex was nice because he wanted to please me.

"Richard was very different. We spoke of philosophy, spirituality, and reincarnation. We talked about ideas, and he excited my mind first. But soon I found myself responding to him physically, feeling the excitement build up. I wanted him to hold my hand, I wanted him to kiss me. I wanted *him*. I was a married lady—I'd never looked at another man—but when Richard came along I was very willing. I would not have broken up the marriage. But I would have become involved with him sexually. I wanted to. The trouble is: that's not what he wanted.

"He lived on a very spiritual level. He said he cared for me very much, but for him having a sexual relationship with a married woman would have placed him on a lower spiritual plane. And he would not allow our relationship to deteriorate. Therefore, we never had sex. Not once during the whole two year affair."*

She looks at me quizzically.

"Does that mean he doesn't qualify as a lover for your book? Is sex a requirement? Because if it is, I can go on to my next lover. My second lover was pure pleasure, although he cost me thousands."

I assure her I want to hear the whole story, so she continues telling me about Richard.

"There was a group of people studying with him. He was sort of our guru. He had studied the Eastern religions and I found it fascinating to hear him speak. I hung on his words. Throughout married life all I ever heard was: 'Where are you going for dinner?';

---

*Nonsexual love affairs are not unknown. For example, Maxwell Perkins' unique love affair with Elizabeth Lemmon was sustained through personal correspondence over 25 years.

or 'What did you buy at Saks?' Very prosaic, everyday things. This boy opened up a whole world for me and I realized how hungry I was for intellectual conversation.

"He was also very good-looking. Until you heard him talk, you'd think he was just another pretty-boy type. But once he opened his mouth, you were in his spell. He had charisma. He was small in stature, but beautiful. He had tremendous dark brown eyes, a beautiful spiritual face like Jesus, and beautiful black wavy hair. He even began to grow a beard. He definitely was not ordinary looking.

"He was a fine musician, he played the flute. And he sculpted and drew. I'd never met anybody like him. He held lectures in New York on Sundays. He lectured on theosophy and philosophy, and the central idea was reincarnation of the soul. He gave me literature to read on 'What Is Death?' and I started to read Plato.

"From that moment on, I wasn't the contented little suburban housewife anymore. From the moment Richard came into my life, the marriage was doomed.

"For 16 years I was content. But always I wished that my husband was a little more intellectual. Whenever I went to a lecture and heard someone speak eloquently, I wished my husband had that capacity for communication. Maybe it was an immature notion on my part—nobody is perfect—maybe I should have judged him on his own merits. He was in the dress business, a successful manufacturer and financially we were well off, comfortable.

"Or maybe I married too young. I was just a kid, I wasn't mature. I needed someone to take care of me. My father died when I was three. My mother remarried when I was five.

"I remember saying before the wedding, 'I don't know if I love you enough,' and my husband said, 'I love you enough for both of us.' He was 22, and that pleased my romantic soul. He was in the army and we would travel from camp to camp. I liked that idea because I wanted to get out of Brooklyn. I'd never been more than five blocks from home. So it seemed a glamorous and exciting life ahead.

"At the time, my stepfather was sick in the hospital and my mother was working, so I was alone a lot. I wanted to be a teacher. I applied to Hunter College and got in, but I went to work instead. I used to line up the kitchen chairs and 'teach' them, give them names and pass out homework. My mother was busy, so I had no one to guide me. My mother had problems with my brother who was retarded, my stepfather was dying; my mother was just too preoccupied. Oh, she loved me, adored me, but there were so many burdens. I looked around and I wanted something more glamorous for myself.

"For sixteen years of marriage, I never thought about alternatives. I was busy raising children, tending a house, and socializing. We moved from Booklyn to Connecticut. My life seemed full. Our son was a wrestler on the high school team, and our daughter played the piano. She was serious about it, and I loved to listen to her practice. I like music. Even the pop tunes. Sometimes I'd be doing the bills and I'd put on records and dance. I have a very romantic nature, but I'm clear in my thinking. I'm not caught up in fantasies. There were little dissatisfactions, but I never expressed them.

"My husband was a warm man. But I wasn't responsive to him. Part of what happened in my marriage was due to my own stupidity. I don't ever remember nibbling on his ear, and I never initiated sex. No, I used to wait for him, and if he didn't want it I was just as happy to turn over and go to sleep.

"It was Richard who brought me to life. I know I'm capable of passion, that I have a great capacity for loving. It's not how many orgasms you have but the kind of passion that encompasses your whole being. My husband never engaged my whole being. I felt comfortable with him. He pleased me. But he didn't arouse me. And it never occurred to me that my sex life was any less pleasing than anybody else's. I didn't see any great excitement among the couples we knew. I was happy we didn't quarrel. It was a placid relationship. He didn't criticize me, he only tried to please me.

"Richard and I started talking one day in the club and I recognized right away he wasn't a 'dese-dem-dose' person. He was lovely to talk to, and I told him how empty things sometimes seemed. He invited me to a lecture in New York and afterwards we talked until two o'clock in the morning. My husband came looking for me and we had a terrible confrontation when I got home. There was nothing to accuse me of, only talk.

"For the next year I continued to take the train in to these lectures and meet Richard in New York. Then he'd drive me home. That's all it amounted to. Talking. A cup of coffee. Then he started calling me in the afternoon or midweek on his day off and we'd meet at a lecture and end up talking in his car. The most that ever happened was his hand on my knee, a kiss. He asked me if I would leave my husband, and I said no. He would stroke my hair, hold my hand, but nothing else. Had he wanted sex, I would have been happy. *I* wanted it. I wanted terribly to sleep with him. But I could never say it. It was a matter of pride. He was so spiritual, he seemed like a saint, above all that. I thought it might turn him off.

"To cover my bases, I told my husband we were just friends and he was welcome to come to New York with us at any time. I really didn't want him to accept that invitation, and fortunately he never did. Even when I went off with Richard on Sundays, he never said, 'Listen, we're here, we're your family—what are you doing in New York?'

"So it was easy. I'd arrange it while the children were in school. we'd meet at a diner or his house, but he never once made an attempt to sleep with me. I told myself over and over he is a spiritual person, a moral person, he lives by certain principles. That's why he won't touch you. But ironically, he met another woman from the club who was willing to divorce her husband in order to marry him. They have three children together now. I missed him, I missed our conversations, I missed the stimulation of reading books together. I felt sad, alone. But still, you don't give up a home and children and a decent husband lightly.

"Two years later, tragedy struck our house. My daughter died in a car accident. I was 37, and in the shock of my grief I called for him. I said, 'Get him here, I want him here, I want to talk to him.' I needed help to cope with my daughter's death. He knew about death and reincarnation. They didn't call him. Although the pain was terrible for my husband, he tried not to talk about it. He tried to comfort *me*. But the guilt over losing your own child, the games that you play—'What if we hadn't let her go that night?'—only made it worse. It was a bad time for us, and we didn't draw closer because of it. We each did our grieving privately.

"I still think about Richard sometimes. That had I divorced my husband, we would have married. But I don't regret it. I could not have lived a full life with him either. I was very involved with being Jewish. I care very much about Israel and the Jewish people, and he was so far removed from that background, so into Eastern religions, I wouldn't have been happy with his theosophy. Having Richard for a spiritual lover was good for me. But it was bad for the marriage. Later, when my husband left me, he told me he never felt I loved him from the time I met Richard.

"He was right. Whenever my husband made love to me, I'd pretend it was Richard. I wished it was Richard. It was Richard I wanted. I was only going through the motions at home, but it was Richard I wanted to be with. He was always on my mind. I'd drop anything for him. I was reading certain books for him, going to lectures that captured my mind. And soon I began to sneer at my husband. He would put a cowboy show on television when he came home tired, and I'd say to myself, 'Humpf, that's all he's capable of.' No, it was not good for the marriage. It was destructive. My husband became less and less appealing to me. There were resentments building up on his side, too. At that time, he was afraid to confront me. But years later, he hit me in the face with it.

"Over the years the marriage changed. I don't know exactly when the relationship cooled. I didn't notice because by that time we had another child, after having lost our daughter, and I was very busy with the baby. I hadn't realized he was increasingly remote because I was depressed, too. I couldn't handle the responsibility of having a baby at 41. I suddenly realized I was sitting in the playground with 21-year-old girls and I said, 'What am I doing here? This should be my grandchild.' It was a bad time for me. I felt shaky.

"A month had gone by when I realized this warm and loving man was not interested in sex. So I said to him, 'Hey, since when are we a brother and sister act?' And he said—I'll never forget it—'I don't know how to tell you this, but you don't turn me on anymore.' I turned ice cold. Like someone had put a knife in my heart.

"'Is there anyone else?'

"'No, I'm just not happy with you anymore.'"

It was a devastating blow.

" 'My God, you do this to me now? What am I going to do? Raise a baby alone? Why didn't you do this to me when I was 35 and had a chance to start a new life?'

"I don't think he gave a damn at that point because he already had someone else. And I was too dumb, too trusting. When he'd call from New York and say, 'Honey, I'm tired, should I drive back tonight?' I'd say, 'No, stay in town, get a good night's sleep.' I never in a million years thought he'd find someone else. I was egotistical enough to think he could never care for anybody but me. Smug. Cocky. It was a rude awakening.

"For a year I walked around in a state of . . . I was boggled. He didn't leave, but we had no relations, and I felt like someone hit me over the head. I took care of the baby, but I was barely functioning. We continued to act married socially, but there was nothing between us. We saw the same friends. I didn't tell anyone, I was too . . . I don't know, maybe dazed is the word.

"Then one Thanksgiving on a Florida vacation with the baby, I asked him if there was someone else and did he want a divorce?

" 'There's nobody and I don't want a divorce,' he said.

"I suggested a marriage counselor, but he absolutely refused. I remember sitting on the beach staring out at the ocean, thinking, 'I wish I had the courage to walk out there and keep walking.' After I lost my daughter—she was graduating from high school—I was feeling the same way. I didn't want to live. But then I'd turn to my little boy playing in the sand and I knew he needed me.

"That Florida vacation was a turning point. One day I noticed a very handsome man in the hotel lounge reading the *Times* and I remembered I hadn't picked up my *New York Post*, so I went to get the paper. When I came out, I deliberately walked past him and made some trivial remark.

" 'Sit down,' he said, and I did.

" 'I've been noticing you on the beach. You're cute, a very sexy lady.'

" 'Who, me?' I wasn't feeling like a sexy lady.

" 'I also noticed what good care you take of your little boy. Don't see much of that kind of mothering these days.'

" 'Well, I'm an old-fashioned girl.' And we got to talking.

"He was extremely attractive. He was alone, divorced, and he asked me why my husband wasn't around much. I made some excuse. And then he handed me his card.

"'If you want to see me, just call. I'd sure like to see you.'

"I was so flattered and so excited. And mostly scared. Because when you're married, you're protected by that wedding ring and you feel comfortable with other men. But when you no longer have that, it's a whole other thing. The next day we spoke briefly and later that night at dinner with my husband and another couple, the man was at the bar. He lifted his glass in a gesture of toasting me, and I smiled back.

"I began to feel the excitement of this gorgeous man. I felt aroused. So aroused, so turned on that that night I *forced* my husband to make love to me. I really did, I forced him. I guess he couldn't help it because he's a man. But what he said to me after was so devastating, he set me on a new path.

"'Don't ever make me do that again! I don't want to do what I don't feel!'

"He utterly destroyed me and he left me in Florida and returned home by himself.

"The next morning, I called that man.

"'Do you still want to see me?'

"'Of course I do.'

"'My husband has gone. I'm here alone.'

"That night he came to my suite. My son was asleep in the other room. And within fifteen minutes we were making love. It was exciting because I had never been with another man.

"'Look,' I told him, 'I've been married 27 years, I don't know how to be with another man. I won't know what to do.'

"He laughed. 'I'll show you.'

"But he didn't have to show me. It was good because I was very excited, desperate to be held. I wanted to be appreciated. It wasn't the sex I wanted, it was the physical togetherness.

"And that was the beginning of our affair."

She laughs. Having reported the intimate details, she allows herself to relax and talk more freely. She pours us more coffee and asks if I'd like some fruit.

"Well, let me tell you, that affair cost me a lot of money. It would have been cheaper to walk into the ocean. Because Jim was a con man. He took me for thousands. He used me. He took a lot of money from me. All cash. He was writing a book—so he said—which never got published. He was a nut, a crazy egomaniac. But it was very exciting, I have to admit it.

"I would go into the city. I had a housekeeper, so I was free to leave. I couldn't wait to get to see him. I'd sit in the lobby of his apartment waiting for him, excited about being with him. He was very attractive, very personable, my age, gray-haired, a very handsome man. Six feet tall and a user of women. He'd done this before. He lived off women. Women helped him financially, he's not a successful man. He said he had a fabric business, then he was writing a book, then he had a holding company, then he was in finance."

She laughs gaily now, throws her head back.

"Finance. He sure was. And I was financing him. Thank God I'm laughing. If you don't laugh, you cry."

She is still chuckling, but she goes on with the story.

"He never had any money, always had a deal that fell through, was always in financial trouble. So—I don't know how to explain this—maybe it was sick. I think I was so needing, so lonely, so heartsick that it didn't matter to me. I wanted to make him happy. Also, I realized at that time that there *was* another woman in my husband's life. He was still in my bed, but he couldn't stand the sight of me. He made no move to leave, he didn't want a divorce, he wanted to do nothing. And I was too scared to do anything myself because I was financially comfortable and he was giving me everything.

"But that New Year's he went to Acupulco just before a big party we were going to. I remember feeling rotten. I had bought this new gown and I went to the party and told everyone he was called away on business. New Year's Eve he phoned and said, 'I know this is shitty of me. But I want to wish you a Happy New Year anyway.' It was his guilt talking. When I hung up, I called Jim in New York just to have somebody to talk to.

43

Having It Both Ways

"On Monday when my husband came home, my housekeeper was unpacking his bags and she said, 'So you finally bought one.' Wrapped in plastic was a little yellow bikini, still damp. I didn't confront him. I was too scared. I didn't want the marriage broken. He was still coming home, so there was hope. I couldn't face being abandoned, being left alone. I let things drift. I felt, 'Let him see the yellow bikini: I have Jim.'

"Until one day, going home in the car, he told me he was in love with someone else. I begged him not to leave. I said, 'You can have your girlfriend. Go with her. But don't break up the marriage.' I figured I had a guy, too. 'Come home and take your old lady out once in a while.' I was trying to pass it off lightly.

"'I can't do that, I love her. She's very lonely without me.'

"'What about my loneliness? What about your sons' loneliness?'

"It didn't make a dent. I was so beaten, so scared. A woman alone doesn't feel she's worth anything. I'll try to explain. I felt an individual worth, I felt I had some fine qualities. But this is a two-by-two society. And when you walk alone, your sense of worth is diminished even if you're the most marvelous person in the world. I think most women alone feel that. I felt very lonely. I felt empty in my heart. With a man I felt different. Even if you go for a walk, if you're alone, you're alone. When you're with somebody, it's a whole other feeling. It's sharing. It's a *man's* hand I want to hold. It's a *man* I want to laugh with and cuddle with. It would be easier if I were a lesbian, but it's a *man* I want. I like to flirt, I enjoy that. It confirms my value. That's why I needed Jim. He was a man.

"For a while I allowed my husband to carry on with the other woman. And I continued to see Jim, making love and giving him money. He didn't ask for it, he would just tell me some sad tale and I'd come across with it. I didn't feel he was a gigolo, that I was only getting a paid lover, because I believed he was very fond of me. He said he cared for me in a way he had never cared for anybody. Well . . ."

She purses her lips in annoyance at herself and sighs.

"At the time I didn't want to think about it. I knew he was really no damn good. He was a lousy lover, too, a selfish lover. My husband was a better lover. When Jim was done making love, he'd

44

quickly turn on the television set and light up a cigar. He didn't know about foreplay or afterplay, he only knew about getting on with it. Once I tried to explain and he said, 'Don't work me over, honey, I got so much on my mind.'

"I knew I was crazy, I said to myself they should put you away for this. But I kept seeing him. I just needed to be loved. I needed someone to tell me I was pretty.

"But then it got too expensive. I knew he wasn't a man I could live with. I kept withdrawing money, and my husband never knew because I had the bank books. I met another man who also wanted money, but by this time I was getting smart—nobody was going to get a nickel out of me. There are men out there who are happy to meet a lady who has money and is willing to trade money for love. It's a very common thing. I know three women right now who have given their lovers money. So when I want to console myself for my stupidity, I think of those three women. I gave away the kind of money most people never see in their whole lifetime. So I guess I've paid my dues.

"Legally, I'm still married, the divorce has not come through. Factually, I had it both ways, had a lover and a husband at the same time. But in this world, I don't think you can. Not really. I'm old fashioned, I still believe exclusivity is a requirement for a husband-wife relationship. Eventually, I cheated on Jim, too, when I felt the emotional part was over.

"See, when a woman goes to bed with a man, it's not just sex."

She leans forward and lowers her voice.

"It's not just sticking it in and moving it around and taking it out. Most women, by their very natures become emotionally involved. I had another lover after Jim and I found myself getting emotionally involved with him, too. I began to get possessive about the nights he wasn't with me. I became jealous. I learned something from my affairs. I could not have a relationship with two men at a time. I would feel dirty."

"And I learned something else about sex. If a woman thinks she's frigid or not the passionate type, it may well be the man. There are very few frigid women. But there are plenty of poor lovers. I haven't had 100 men, but you don't have to have 100 to know. It's the man who creates the right atmosphere in the bedroom. Women, by nature, are responders. Maybe it's me, but I like the man to be dominant. Not in a mean, rough way, but I like to be bossed. I find that exciting. Younger women may feel different. If a woman isn't happy with her sex life, she shouldn't blame herself. It sounds like women's lib to say this, but mostly it's the man's fault. Some men are very inept lovers.

"Of course communication is the key. But there are born communicators like there are born lovers and born dancers. What makes a fantastic lover? He knows how to make you laugh. He makes sex fun. It's not doing five minutes of this and five minutes of that. It's turning lovemaking into the most fun thing to do. I didn't know that until I met my present lover. It took me a long time, but it's never too late. Age doesn't matter.

"We do the craziest things together. Nutty things beyond my wildest dreams. Unbelievable. I never would have done it with my husband when I was 20. It's the fun of caressing. Here's one I like. We'd have wine, and he'd pour a little into a very private place."

She wiggles her eyebrows like Groucho Marx.

"Then he'd lick it off. Next, *my* turn. I'd hold my glass of wine and dip him into it. Then *I'd* lick him off. And we'd laugh and laugh. A beautiful man, a very bright man—very knowledgeable about a woman's body. Maybe because he's a biomedical engineer."

She laughs at her own joke, enjoying herself.

"He's a very sensual man. He will bathe me and scrub me and powder me, and then make love to me. Oh God, I've never enjoyed anybody so much in my life. Three and a half years. He's adorable, a nut in his way, but such a fun person. He says our relationship goes between two rooms. He loves to cook. He cooks for me and feeds me in bed. Those are the two rooms: the kitchen and the bedroom."

Just then we hear the door slam.

"It's my son home from school. Please shut off the tape."

She stands up and smoothes her dress.

"I'm in the den, honey."

The interview is over.

❖ ❖ ❖

Each of Ellen's affairs was a response to a particular hunger. Richard, her spiritual lover, satisfied her craving for a life of the mind. She turned to her second lover, Jim, after an explicit sexual rejection by her husband. Perhaps the fact that she had been refused and rejected by two men in succession was too profound a blow to her sense of self; she found herself a lover who turned out to be a gigolo and paid for his sexual favors, although she was unable to accept the situation and its implications for a long time.

Like Ellen, many people get caught up in the business of marriage. Their separate interests and pressing demands replace a genuine exchange of feelings. They talk, but they don't communicate clearly. Conversations become limited to bulletins about the doctor bill, the car payment, and the broken washing machine. Until the emptiness becomes apparent.

Although the two-year affair with Richard did not include sex, Ellen discovered that her mind was her most erogenous zone. By stimulating her mind, he aroused her sexually and released her capacity for passion. He prepared the way for her future affairs.

How can this happen? It seems extraordinary. For Ellen was a woman who had everything: a warm and loving husband, two fine children, a beautiful home, money, status, health, youth. Enough for most wives. Utopia for those in less comfortable marriages. But not enough for Ellen. She had the outward appointments of happiness. But it simply was never enough. Like many women, Ellen was waiting to be engaged at a deeper level, to be "brought to life," to feel that all of her being had finally come into play. She was still, in some sense, a virgin in a deep sleep.

Once Ellen talked to Richard, she was never the same. Richard got hold of her mind. She compares him to Jesus. Some therapists subscribe to a theory which they call "scripting." Most women marry "the right person," someone who fits the "script." His religion is right, his class, his appearance, his education—everything about him says GO. Then years later, they fall in love with someone

47

else—head over heels, with somebody who appears to be the most unlikely candidate. They are meeting their own needs, not the script that was written for them.

Many wives report their love affair helped them tolerate an unsatisfactory marriage. Others claim having a lover helped them find the strength to break up the marriage. However, Ellen's affair with Richard spelled the end of her comfortable marriage. Now the marriage became intolerable.

"From that moment on, I wasn't the same contented little suburban housewife. From the moment Richard came into my life, the marriage was doomed." In Ellen's case, her lover was compared to her husband. Each pleasure with her lover only underscored her husband's deficiencies. So the split widened. Ellen admits Richard was not good for the marriage, that her husband became less and less appealing.

To Ellen's credit, she does not blame the demise of her marriage solely on her husband. She recognizes that the crisis of losing their daughter did not bring them closer. Having a baby at 41 made her resentful. Instead of overcoming the joint problem, it only widened the breach. His affair came as a devastasting conclusion to a marriage she had assumed was invulnerable. It had never occurred to her that her husband could also find a lover. She was frightened. She wanted to keep the marriage together. Having another baby, perhaps to replace her lost daughter, had not provided her with comfort. Nor had that third child cemented the marriage. Instead she became depressed, felt overwhelmed by responsibilities, and frustrated by her husband's increasing remoteness. She could not face being abandoned and left alone. Yet she and her husband were leading separate lives. There was no communication with him.

Loneliness—the absence of communication—is a powerful motivation. Joyce Carol Oates knew it:

> It's bad for you to be alone, to be lonely, because if aloneness does not lead to God, it leads to the devil. *

Was Richard her god?
Was Jim her devil?

*From Joyce Carol Oates's story "Shame" in *Wheel of Love and Other Stories.*

Ellen will soon be divorced. Her problems began years back when all seemed like Camelot in Connecticut. Certainly there are many factors, never one, that paved the way for this divorce. However, inability to communicate was a large element.

❋   ❋   ❋

I interviewed Donna in her small home outside Philadelphia. It was a typical split level in a row of look-alikes, part of a large housing development. The paint on the outside of the house was chipped and the railing was peeling. She stood on the front stoop holding her dark lacquered hair in place against the wind—a solemn, unsmiling reserve about her.

Donna was 46, married 26 years when Adolfo and she became lovers. He was her tennis instructor and ten years younger than she.

"Never, never again would I get involved with a married man. When you go out with a married man, no matter what he says—even if he's separated—he'll go back to his wife. A man and a woman can go into an affair and say it's strictly sex, but a woman is going to get emotionally involved. I did. But we never said we loved each other.

"I knew Adolfo for many years. He always appealed to me. But he flirted wildly with all the women he coached so I never took him up on his remarks, though I knew they were meant to turn me on. But the timing was right, and I was ready.

"I hadn't slept with my husband for ten years. I had completely turned myself off, taken sex out of my life.* For years I didn't do anything about it. If I needed to satisfy myself, I masturbated. For years I was so cold I felt nothing. Oh, a few brief affairs, of no importance. I had no confidence in myself for a real love affair.

"I was 36. My marriage was over. We stayed together for two reasons: the four kids—I loved them so much—and money. What keeps us together now is also money—a lack of it. No money for a divorce and all it involves. I know all about divorce and I'm scared to death of it.

"Divorce is a horrible experience. My parents were divorced when I was 11. I went to live with my mother and I hated it. I felt discriminated against. My friends tapered off because I was the child of a divorced woman—this was in the forties. My father was a

---

*Donna discusses this later.

49

weak man and he'd come on Sundays to cry to us: 'Please try to get us back together, I'm nothing without your mother.' And to this day, I hate Sundays and holidays. It meant my father was coming, and it meant tears.

"For 17 years my husband has worked for the same trucking company. He's the best for what he does, but he gets nothing for it. He demands nothing. So it's been a struggle for money all our lives.

"When it was time for our son to go to college, I went to work. My husband made no plans. 'If you don't have the money, you don't go,' he said. He's a very passive man. His parents were divorced, too. His father's been married three times. So has my mother. My husband was also married once before me and has two other kids, but he never sees them—or his five grandchildren.

"I think he has guilt feelings about it, but he's a man who doesn't communicate. He's never allowed himself to think about himself. He believes that if you don't see something, it will go away. My husband sees only what he wants and avoids confrontation. He says there's nothing in the world worth fighting over. So we don't argue because there's no communication. No companionship. No sex. We lead separate lives. We never have an argument.

"No, that's not true. We once had a big blow-up. It was over money. He comes from a wealthy family, and he feels there's nothing to worry about because there's going to be money eventually. He forgets that by the time you inherit money, you're past raising kids. We had a big fight, but he wouldn't confront the issues. I started screaming at the top of my lungs. I was hysterical, almost fainting. He had to smack me across the face. And *still* nothing changed. It was the most frustrating thing in the world. Maybe I wanted that smack. It was better than his silence.

"The crazy thing is that in the beginning my husband was a fantastic lover. He could have been a professional. Our marriage was not based on love, it was based on sex. But that was a powerful bond, especially in the beginning. I always had orgasms with him. I learned everything about sex from him because I had never slept with anyone before. I was a virgin at twenty-three. He was twenty-seven, an older man to me, and there was nothing that wasn't exciting with him. I never had any inhibitions about what could be done—because he was my husband. We had oral sex, anal sex—which I didn't like—but everything else went. Until he introduced

50

wife-swapping. I felt terrible that he needed another woman. What wasn't he getting from me? I started to get ill from it. I actually developed ulcers. But I went along because I knew he wanted it.

"It was with some good friends of ours. We met and became friends very quickly, and my husband talked to me about switching. I didn't think he meant it, but he did.

"He enjoyed it, but it disturbed me terribly. I got nothing out of sex with this other man. What made it worse was that we did it in their house and in our house—with the children around. I felt so uneasy and ashamed—suppose my children knew. Everyone said we were perfect parents.

"Married 13 years and that was the end of the marriage. A few stabs over the years at making up, but it was dead. I was only 36. In my mind my marriage was over. No more sex. It was settled. I wanted a divorce, but he wouldn't give it to me. I refused to sleep with him. So we wound up in separate bedrooms.

"For the next ten years I held off. A man here and there, a little escapade, but nothing important. I was afraid to try a real affair. I didn't know how you go about it.

"I kept putting it off and putting it off, and frustrating myself, finding excuse after excuse to say no. But I wanted an affair, I wanted a man very badly. I even went to a therapist, but it didn't help. I was depressed all the time.

"Then Adolfo came into the picture. He played it cool, he really did. He had lovers throughout his marriage and he was very experienced.

"He made me feel comfortable. He talked to me. It wasn't love, I know that. I guess it started with sex. But it was the closeness with somebody I craved. You won't believe this—maybe you will—sex was not the most important part for me. As much as I felt for him, as much as he turned me on, I never had an orgasm with him. Not once. I used to come home and think about it and wonder why. It's strange. I was very happy making love *without* orgasms. I mean I enjoyed it so much, he probably never knew. I felt satisfied without it. Also I was afraid it would turn him off if he knew, maybe he wouldn't feel masculilne. I like to be held, no, I *love* to be held. I could just lay in his arms, that was important to me. He talked to me. He listened to me. Even though he had no children, I could talk to him about mine.

"What got me into an affair? A chance to talk to somebody. Companionship. Communication. Although the affair lasted only a year, it was wonderful. I enjoyed it so much. Being with Adolfo, talking with him, I learned a lot.

"I knew it couldn't go on forever. I was married, he was married.

"At first I felt insecure about our age difference. But he said it was ridiculous. I asked him if he would be embarrassed to be seen with a woman ten years older, and he said not at all. I was very nervous about it—scared my kids or their friends might see us. After all, I had grown kids and many of their friends knew me.

"Adolfo told me to meet him in a particular parking lot. I'd wait for him there and quickly jump into his car. Then we'd go straight to a motel.

"We had such good times. We'd talk and we'd laugh over our childhood. We could tell each other all the funny things that happened. And he'd explain his plans to start his own indoor club. He's a very ambitious person; that's something I love. Very well dressed. God, how I enjoyed that man!

"Maybe his ambition turned me on because my husband had no ambition. I admire a person who has ambition, dreams, but isn't showy. He had wonderful plans and we'd talk about them.

"He'd get in touch with me by calling the hospital where I did volunteer work five days a week. A short message: where to meet and when.

"At first I was frightened. I hadn't had sex for so long. But you don't forget."

She pushes her chair back and busies herself serving mugs of hot coffee and a plate of sliced pound cake. She is trying to cover her embarrassment.

"My husband was having his flings, too. Whenever he went out of town on business, he had women. His main office was in the midwest and I remember getting a phone call once at three in the morning from a woman who said, 'Your husband just left my bed. How do you feel about that?' It sort of bothered my ego, but all I could think of was: does she realize it's three o'clock in the morning? When I confronted him, he denied it. 'Somebody's trying to make trouble for me,' he said, 'and I thought everybody liked me.'

"As my affair with Adolfo went on, I felt less and less guilty. It didn't hurt anybody and it gave me such pleasure. Why feel guilty? As far as my husband was concerned, it didn't change anything. He didn't love me. I was a convenience. I kept his house clean. I raised his children, and I took all the major problems off his hands. I was also the best mother I knew how to be. And God knows I didn't have much of a guide from *my* mother.

"My mother was very cold to me. My father wasn't around. My mother never kissed me or held me. I never remember being kissed by my mother.

"That's why I wanted to get married at 20. I used my husband to get what I wanted. To be a mother. To have children and a home of my own. I wanted to raise the perfect family.

"We have no friends together. We lead separate lives. I don't want to go out with him socially. I don't want to sleep with him. I want nothing to do with him. I see a few women—my sister mostly—for lunch or shopping. There's no companionship.

"My sister is lucky. She has a husband who talks. I guess I'm jealous of her in that way. He talks to her about everything. He's a cop and he entertains her with all his stories. He trusts her. 'I'm one of the few people he trusts,' she told me. 'He can let it all out with me. I'm a sounding board for him.' God, how I envy that kind of closeness!

"My husband doesn't give a damn what I do. So naturally, there's no checking up, and that makes it easy for me to have an affair. Adolfo would call once a week. We didn't talk much on the phone, we just set the date. But when we were together, we would discuss anything, everything. Television shows, movies, what's happening in the papers.

"But I guess I became too possessive. I never told him so, but I wanted more and more of him. I wanted to see him more often, to share more of our lives. He had feelings for me, too. But not as strong as mine.

"A man can sleep with a woman without emotional involvement. But women want more. This is the makeup of a woman. I don't know what kind of woman can sleep with somebody with no involvement. A one-night stand maybe. But if you're having an affair, you become emotionally involved.

"I felt depressed when it was over. Abandoned, again. But I

53

knew the signs, typical signs. His calls got less frequent. The love-making changed. At first it was three times a night. Then once. Toward the end of the year, he seemed less interested, in a hurry to leave, so he found an excuse to go. I never spent a night with him. I always came right home. It was understood: the affair was limited to sex. He wanted no real emotional involvement. When it was over, it was over.

"Maybe there's a built-in, self-destruct when both parties are married. I don't know. My situation was different from his. My marriage was over; his was alive. He had friends, interests—he knew how to fit an affair into his life and go on. Before we even went to bed, we had this understanding: It would last as long as it lasted. Those were the ground rules and we both accepted them. It hurt and sometimes I felt used, but I knew what I was getting into. I needed a relationship. Someone to talk to.

"Well, the affair is over. And I'm locked into my marriage economically. It's too much of a hassle to start from scratch. The pure hard facts are that we stay together for economic necessity. I love my comforts. My washer and dryer. I thought of that. Living alone in an apartment, divorced—what would I have?

"The affair gave me strength. So there are no hard feelings. Even when I saw the end coming, I couldn't allow myself to get mad. I found I was staying around waiting for his phone call, and then he stopped calling. I felt empty. I had enjoyed the physical contact, the sex. But most of all, I missed having that something extra in my life. I felt lonely again.

"What brought it to an end? Time. Just time. We never talked about it, but we broke up friends. I still go to the club to take lessons.

"I take courses. I go to work. But that's not the answer. You can't go to bed with your job or your degree. You need intimacy and closeness. I could have a million in the bank and still need a man. That's my makeup. I need to touch, to hold hands, to communicate and talk.

"I don't know what's going to happen. There's no communication with my husband. And it's all over with Adolfo. Maybe I'll get lucky. Maybe another man'll come along. Like the song says, maybe someday he'll come along, the man I love, and he'll be big and strong . . ."

Donna sits there. Silent. Glum. She is waiting for a man to rescue her as the song promises. Of all the women I interviewed, Donna was the one who never laughed.

❀   ❀   ❀

Donna and her husband remain married. But for the paucity of communication between them, they may as well be divorced. Sexually, socially, emotionally—they lead separate lives.

Donna says her marriage is lacking *communication*. Therapists term it psychic intimacy. It is the sense of closeness and sharing between people, and extreme deprivation can cause depression. Donna may have recognized this when she went to a therapist for help.

Depression is much more common among women than it is among men. Is it because women have a greater need for intimacy?

Many researchers over the past ten years have been convinced that women are more interested in "relationships" than men are.* Female babies—as young as two days old—seem more responsive to other human begins than male babies. Later, the girls seem to smile and babble more. Dr. Helen Block Lewis, in her book *Psychic War in Men and Women,* points out that women show greater sensitivity than men. And the culture which casts them in the role of caretakers seems to emphasize this.

Closeness is vital for normal functioning. People suddenly cut off from a human being upon whom they have depended suffer deep, aching loneliness. Lynn Caine's book *Widow* tells of her struggle to become a whole person again after the death of her husband.

Divorced people suffer similar pain. However bad the marriage may have been, they find the adjustment to their initial loneliness very difficult.

"For months after we broke up and he moved out, I couldn't handle the loneliness," a young teacher said. "The kids kept me busy and I kept going. But I needed someone to talk to, someone out there to listen to me. The four walls were driving me crazy. I *missed* the bastard! Even though I kept telling myself I was well rid of him, the loneliness got to me. I was depressed."

In a humorous article called "The Roadbed's Bumpy Without a

*Maggie Scarf makes these points in *Unfinished Business.*

Having It Both Ways

Coupling,"* Charlotte Perkins discusses loneliness after separating, and she admits, "I missed you." She says, "I never thought much about the ark until my husband and I separated. Now I look around me and see pairs everywhere."

The loneliness experienced by widowed, divorced, and separated women is understandable. However, marriage by itself does not immunize a person against loneliness. If the partners are leading separate lives, like Donna and her husband, if there is no love, no sex, no communication, the pain and depression of loneliness can be equally intense.

Prisoners have demonstrated how depressed and apathetic they become when deprived of human contact. And children reared with a minimum of loving, stroking, and talking often fail to develop normally. Studies show that monkeys who are deprived of contact with a mother figure or other monkeys do not develop properly. Communication is esssential to normal growth and normal functioning.

In our depersonalized society of answering machines and computers, opportunities for human contact decrease, and emotional closeness with a caring spouse becomes more and more essential. Cut off from emotional satisfaction, Donna sought relief outside marriage in Adolfo. The affair supplied the companionship she didn't have in her marriage.

While Donna's story illustrates an extreme breakdown in communication, the number of married couples leading separate lives may be far more common than we suspect. It is an irony that such couples are counted as married in the U.S. Census.

As the soaring divorce rate testifies, couples separate more easily today. Working women are no longer financially dependent on their husbands. Today if a woman is deprived of close communication, if financial and sexual problems seem overwhelming, she is not likely to turn herself off and masturbate for ten years as Donna did. Nor is she likely to wait around for "Mr. Right" to rescue her. Many women today take matters into their own hands. One of the options is to divorce.

"I couldn't believe it," the stockbroker said. "Nancy and I would

*The New York Times, August 3, 1980.

spend hours discussing our college crowd, who had the good marriages, and who was splitting. I was feeling pretty smug. We lived the good life. We had money, friends, a lot of satisfaction in our lives. Then one day—out of nowhere—my wife of eleven years says: 'It's finished, over.' And she wants me to get out. Just like that. No warning. She drops the bomb. *Boom!*"

"'What are you talking about? What's the matter?' But I was whistling in the dark. I knew she meant business. I could have died.

"'Hold it. Let's talk about it,' I pleaded.

"'No. Too late. The marriage is over. Didn't you hear the bell ring?' She wouldn't talk about it."

Another woman, mother of two small boys, reported the same experience when she told her husband they were finished.

"Why can't we talk about it?" he begged.

"The time for talk is over."

Apparently, the tolerance level among most younger couples has dropped.

"Kids today don't try as hard as we did," is a common lament among long-married couples who are bothered by the rising divorce rate. "We worked on our marriage," they brag, "but the minute one little thing doesn't go their way, they throw in the towel." Why? Perhaps in part because divorce is an acceptable option today.

A prominent family court judge, John R. Mulligan, says that lack of communication is the root cause of divorce in this country. Some therapists agree. They say troubled couples don't express themselves clearly or frequently; they don't wrestle with their problems, which then blow up into major confrontations. The person who argues over every small point may be foolish, but the spouse who refuses to talk courts disaster. Silence is often used as a weapon. It breeds hostility and aggravates irritations. Donna developed ulcers. Psychosomatic illnesses are well documented in the medical literature. The inability to articulate one's psychological discomforts is often transmitted into physiological problems. Lack of communication, like a vitamin deficiency, could be the cause.

Wives who are contemplating an outside relationship often seek a specific communication: "No, you can't." Many women express resentment when their husband fails to "stop" them from entering an affair. Both Donna and Ellen took the initial step and their husbands did not object. Ellen spent Sundays with Richard, a day normally reserved for families, and Donna said, "My husband doesn't give a damn." A subconscious resentment sets in when a husband fails to "check up" and communicate his displeasure over a prospective suitor. A wife may feel: "If he doesn't care what I do, I'll show him."

Can communication reestablish a faltering relationship?

Some couples can articulate their problems. Others overcommunicate but do not communicate well.

Then there are the silent communicators. The ones who administer a sharp kick under the dining room table, or a penetrating stare to make their point. A gesture, a glance, a crossing of arms sends a clear message. Every woman who has ever flirted knows a smile can say, "Hi, I'd like to know you better." A glint in the eye can communicate, "I'm available. Are you?"

"I was furious at Kenny at the office Christmas party," a young wife said. "Everytime Barbara came up to him and flirted, he lapped it up. 'It was nothing,' he said. It was just the way he cooed and looked so pleased. I could have killed him. The sexy little bitch was coming on to my husband, and was he enjoying it!"

Some couples are so busy talking, they don't bother to listen. They talk *at* each other, *across* each other, and *about* each other. But they don't communicate. Linda Bird Franke reports* on a solidly married couple who lent their shoulders to squabbling married friends, listened to their complaints, and then concluded: "There was no correlation between the husband's and the wife's stories. It was as if they were in separate marriages. The wife had one marriage. The husband another."

Today, a big word is honesty. An honest relationship. Honest communications. Honest disagreements. Honesty seems to promise its own rewards. However, those into the lay-it-all-out-on-the-table school often mistake quantity for quality in communications. They tell all with abandon and expect to be rewarded. "Haven't I been honest? Isn't that what you want—honesty?" They don't

The New York Times, November 17, 1977.

recognize that too much communication can be as damaging as too little. As psychologist Dr. Joyce Brothers told her television audience, often there is more communication the year before the divorce than any other time.

Overcommunicating—dragging out every hurt, recalling every wound, and peeling away every scab—can cause damage. Truth-telling is not the same as confession. Wives who feel compelled to uncover all the details of an affair (past or present) are taking a big chance. In relieving their own guilt, they may inflict tremendous damage. There are very few husbands who can take a confession of infidelity and not feel wounded. Husbands may say, "I don't care what you did, just tell me the truth." But when it is all laid out on the table, they are mortified.

Even issues far less threatening than a love affair do not demand total honesty.

"When I asked my husband how he rated me on a scale of 1 to 10, I said I wanted the truth. I demanded it! 'Tell me exactly how you'd feel if you saw me walk into your office right now. Not your wife, a total stranger.' Well, he gave it to me! Wiped me out. What did I need to hear all that for? 'Too chubby,' he said. 'Should lose ten pounds.' I know, I'm trying. 'Hair messy, needs a cut and a new style.' My hands, my legs, my breasts—he went over every inch of me. All along I thought of myself as an 8. It was devastating to know my own husband rated me only a 6. Total honesty—who needs it? He hurt my feelings. But I have to admit I asked for it."

Sometimes total honesty can backfire.

"When we came home from the party, I wanted Alex to tell me I was right about an argument I had with another woman over a movie we'd seen. I wanted him to say she acted like a fool and that I was the one who came off looking good. I was still smoldering because I *knew* she'd got the better of me. 'So what do you think?' I asked him. 'Tell me the truth. Be honest.'

" 'Well, there's two sides to every question,' he tried to sidestep it.

" 'No, c'mon, tell me. Don't dodge it.'

" 'Let's go to sleep, hon, I'm beat.'

" 'Alex! I want the truth. You can tell me."

" 'Okay, okay. You sounded like a jerk. A Class One jerk.' I could have killed him. When he tried to make love to me later, I turned

59

my back to him and his goddam honesty. I didn't talk to him for two days.'

On the other hand, Amy, a young feminist, told me this.

"Communication? We agree on nothing! Sometimes I wonder how we ever got married. My husband is a gardener, a macho Italian gardener. I thought we had the same values and cared about the same things. But after twelve years it turns out we don't. I changed. He didn't. I'm for legal abortions and he's against it. When I became pregnant again and wanted an abortion, I needed his signature. He wouldn't give it to me, and the fight was on. I joined a consciousness-raising group and marched for legalized abortion. I carried a placard:

> Not the church
> Not the State
> Women must
> Decide their fate.

which made him livid. I *got* the abortion. And he carried on like God was going to strike me dead. I didn't want a third child after two kids in three years. I wanted a rest. What's worse for a child than to be unwanted? *That's* the real crime.

"Now we don't agree on anything. Not on music, not politics, nothing. We have a list of subjects we *don't* talk about. The best communication for us is no communication."

This marriage can hardly last.

Some men become irate when their wives refuse to obey them. *Beyond the Male Myth* by Anthony Pietropinto and Jacqueline Simenauer makes the point that well-educated men and men in the younger age brackets are *less* likely to complain about independent women. These men turn to women for closeness and communication. They value women as companions and view them as equals. The woman who can communicate is highly prized.

What do younger men want? Most men wanted a woman concerned with their needs, an affectionate and sincere partner. To the question "What besides love would be your main reason for getting married?" half answered companionship. One man said: "Companionship is a solution to alienation and loneliness."

Men under 35 reflected the permissive society—at least toward themselves. There was "a very definite trend toward infidelity among younger men," perhaps because their needs were not being met at home. However, whether that permissiveness is extended to their wives is doubtful.

Women under 35 still value romance and the man who can communicate his feelings.

"For me actions speak louder than words," a 28-year-old librarian said. "My husband is a Ph.D. in Victorian literature, and he has a brilliant vocabulary. Everyone marvels at his letters. Even his interoffice memos are a treat. People at the university save them for their humor and style and pass them around. But when the man communicates with *me*, he is a different person. I don't mean his vocabulary fails him, he's a very verbal man. What I mean is he isn't a toucher. I've told him how much I'd like it if he'd hold my hand in the movies or kiss me goodbye in the morning. But he only laughs. All I'm asking for is a touch on the shoulder, a hug, a squeeze. My husband is a superb lover in bed. But outside the bedroom, he never takes me in his arms or kisses me. And that would communicate more to me than all his fancy words."

A bright young bookkeeper told me a happier story. "When I talk to other women, I realize how lucky I am. My husband is a very physical guy and I just love it. He's always smooching my ears or stroking my arm or touching me in tender little ways that communicate how he feels. He doesn't wait for intercourse to get amorous. With him, touching is not a means to an end. It's just his way of telling me how he feels."

Terry Schultz in *Bittersweet* says: "After I left my husband, I slept with men more for the affection than the sex, although the sex was often good just the same. I enjoyed the orgasms but needed the touching and holding."

Like Donna, people panicked by loneliness may be driven to sexual encounters in the mistaken belief that sex is the ultimate communication. They confuse sex with intimacy. But when sex is pursued out of loneliness, it can end with emptiness. Good sex can be the most intimate communication a couple can experience— when it is the fulfillment of a loving relationship.

Hostility: Ada

"COME TO MY apartment," she said. "Tomorrow. We'd better do this fast. Before I get cold feet."

I reached Ada through a friend of a friend. When I assured her on the telephone that no one—not even the transcriber who would be typing up the tapes—would know her identity, she agreed to meet me.

Who was she?

Ada was plump, dark-haired, vivacious, with her hands constantly gesturing. Open, articulate, smiling, she disarmed me completely. She seemed to be bursting with energy. She was 36, and the mother of two boys, seven and ten, when she took a lover.

"I have an extraordinary amount of energy. It's nervous energy. But when I met Larry [her lover], I was physically and emotionally depleted. There was nothing left.

"I had had anal surgery, and at the same time I had injured my right hand. Since I'm a court stenographer—sitting and typing all day—well [she tried to joke] I was hurting at both ends. When I came home from the hospital, I found the dishes undone for the week I was gone, the house was an absolute mess, and the laundry was waiting for me. Arthur had fed the kids, nothing else. They were almost out of clothes, and here I was with my hand in a cast. I needed him and he wasn't there for me. I think he expected me to come home from the hospital and get right back to work. He wouldn't allow me time to recover. I felt so let down, so disappointed. I could taste the anger in the back of my throat. I'm the type of person who will keep swallowing hard, but the knot in my throat just wouldn't go away. I wanted to hit him.

"On top of that, we had a fire in the house. He had shoved a huge piece of wood into the fireplace, it hit the damper, and we had $3,000 in repair bills. The money wasn't a problem—the insurance took care of it. But the inconvenience, coming on top of my being unable to function, pushed me closer to the line.

"But it was Arthur's total lack of empathy that finally sent me into another man's arms. I was hurt. I felt short-changed. I wanted a man who would be there to comfort me.

"Here I was running a 50-hour-a-week job—and often I brought home extra typing—plus a house, two little kids, and a husband who did little to help.

"We'd fight over my reading in bed. I used to read all the time, and my husband resented it. He felt the bed was for sex or for sleeping. Sometimes he'd scream at me and I'd go into my son's room to finish the chapter in peace.

"The hostility was building up for years. I used to say to myself, 'When the kids grow up, I'll have my own bedroom so I can read a book in bed and he won't scream at me.'

"But it was what happened 5 or 6 weeks after surgery that pushed me over the edge.

"I woke up one night to find my sexually frustrated husband on top of me, inside me—it was rape the way I looked at it. I hemorrhaged the next day and had to be given two pints of blood. The doctor couldn't understand what had happened and I was too ashamed to tell him the truth. It wasn't only the physical pain, which in itself was considerable, but the pain of knowing that he was only concerned with his own need for sex. The stitches were still healing and I felt so weak and damaged. Then the rape. I felt violated. It put me back for months.

"Looking back, sex with Arthur was never great. You see, my husband had no experience before me. We were very young when we got married. I was 19 and he was 23. He was a virgin. Imagine. A Ph.D. and a virgin! *I* was the experienced one. I had had a lover before I married Arthur. While making love I'd tell him, 'If you want to really excite me, play around with my breasts.' He never touched me around the vagina and we never had oral sex. One fast touch and he was ready to leap. It was all too fast for me. His idea of foreplay was a dab at my breast and right to work. And if we didn't have sex every couple of days he was very unhappy.

"Arthur was an altogether unhappy person, and I felt sorry for him. He hated his job—he was a chemist for a pharmaceutical company—he hated his boss, and he hated his life. Sex was . . . well, his only relief. If he didn't have sex—like when I was pregnant the second time—he was a zombie. What it came down to was I was servicing him. Periodically I would say, 'Hey listen. Wait a minute. Count to 100.' But then I'd let him go ahead. I would have sex with him and go right back to my typing.

"I thought about leaving him. But where would I go? I was scared that I couldn't survive on my own. I had two small children and very little money. Even though I was working that would never have been enough to support the three of us. Before I made a move I had to be self-supporting. That's what held me back. I wanted to be a super mother, do right by my children. I didn't want to be the cause of their suffering.

"Money was one of our problems, too. Arthur had an obsession about making more money. A couple of times he put money into the market, but he lost every cent—even what we set aside to pay my estimated taxes. His salary was $23,000—not enough even with my help.

"After awhile I turned into his mother. No, wrong. I was his mother, his father, his uncle, his sister—everyone. His mother had died and his father gave up on him, so he clung to me. He didn't like to be with people. He wouldn't even go shopping unless I dragged him out. He'd wear one black shoe and one brown shoe unless I laid his clothes out for him. He wouldn't look in the mirror, and he walked slumped over. You know the type? They never look at you when they talk. I knew he didn't like himself, and I felt sorry that he couldn't have a better opinion of himself. I couldn't stand his touch.

"He had a way of pinching me and saying, 'You need a little less weight here. A little bit more there.' Sure I was a little overweight—ten pounds, no more. I never weighed over 140. But in the midst of lovemaking, he'd give me a pinch and say, 'A little too much here.'

"Then Larry came along [she sighs]. And he was an oasis. He made me feel sylphlike, beautiful, brilliant.

"He was a successful attorney—I met him in court—sharp, very much in charge of himself. He dressed beautifully, was well put together, and wore a delicious cologne. He was past 40, and maybe into his own male menopause—who knows? But he was funky and off-beat, and I admired the marvelous way he had with words.

"We were sitting around and talking one day with the reporters, and he said, 'I like the way you talk.' I remember that moment. I felt so flattered because it was coming from a man like that. Here was this fantastically attractive attorney telling me that *I* had a way with words.

"I started seeing him casually. A cup of coffee, a drink. And he began to say he'd like a relationship that included bed. Well, I knew he was married and had kids, so I thought it was ridiculous. I told him, 'Leave me alone, I've got enough problems.'

"But from that moment on, something wonderful entered my life. Everything took on special meaning.

"I began to notice everything about him. His eyes, which were deep brown, his hair, kind of Afro style, and his hands—large and strong. Above all his walk. A confident stride. I loved the way he moved. In court, I couldn't take my eyes off him. And in retrospect, it was a state of consciousness that turned everything sunny. Golden.

"Did I feel guilty about meeting Larry after work? I did. I felt guilty and nervous and scared—really scared. I had never arranged to meet a man secretly during my marriage.

"But my hostility was building against my husband. Anger works in a funny way. It stamps out the guilt, some of it anyway. You want to hit back.

"First you say, 'No, I couldn't.' But then you figure why shouldn't you have something for yourself? All I got at home was pain. Don't I deserve a little relief? A little pleasure for myself?

"One day Larry telephoned and came to my apartment. I don't

know what finally flung me into bed with him, but I thought, 'Well, why not?' And right there in my son's room we made love. That was the room I escaped to when I wanted to read.

"After that, it wasn't hard to meet. He was able to come to my place during the day when no one was home.

"Sex wasn't that great in the beginning. As long as it was happening in my house, I didn't feel I was really having an affair. And that relieved some of my guilt.

"Everything changed when I came back from vacation. The day I went to a motel with him, the relationship changed. I felt free. I was going out of my house to be with him. Now we could take our stolen moments anywhere. When I walked out the door to meet him, I found an oasis amid the realities of my life. At that point I said to myself 'the hell with Arthur.' I had a lover. Life was wonderful.

"The love affair seemed to give me energy—I had so much energy it was unbelievable. I could work all day long, type 100 pages, meet my lover, take care of the house and my kids, even service my husband. I got a lot of practice putting on different hats. I'd be a wife, a mommy, an employee, a lover. And I was so even tempered all during that time, my husband said he never had it so good. If it weren't for Larry, I wouldn't have been able to handle my life. The divorce would have come years earlier. I'm convinced my lover made my marriage bearable. It uncorked some of the hostility and anger. Having a lover was like having my own private psychologist—with a little act in bed to top it off.

"It was glorious. Larry was terrific in bed. He freed me sexually. He introduced me to oral sex. I remember the first time. I lay there feeling like I do when I'm in stirrups for my vaginal exam. My hands were gripping the sides of the sheets, but I figured I ought to try it. I'm glad I did.

"Larry was never clumsy or clinical the way my husband was. Arthur would bring home *The Joy of Sex*, for instance, plop it in the middle of the bed, and say, 'Okay. Now put your leg there. No, two inches over.' Clinical. Not tender or romantic.

"And could Larry talk. That man knew how to communicate. If I said, 'I feel like hell,' he'd say, 'Tell me,' and I could tell him. He helped me understand my feelings and he gave me a chance to change what I said or clarify it. It made me feel free. He was a great listener, he wasn't judgmental, he was patient. He let me talk.

"No matter what I told him, he thought I was wonderful. When we'd go off for a day, we'd go to a motel and we'd have sex two or three times. And he'd say, 'Wow! With you it still works.' Also, he wasn't jealous about my sleeping with my husband. Sometimes he'd ask, 'How was last night?' And I'd answer, 'I fell asleep easily.' Which meant I hadn't had sex with Arthur.

"It went on for two years that way. Idyllic. We joined a theater group together. It was an excuse to see more of each other. He had a beautiful voice. We went to rehearsals together, did a few numbers together. By then I was earning $12,000.

"Then one day he called me at home. One sentence: '*She just found out.*' Then he hung up. His wife issued an ultimatum. And we decided to cool it.

"I was feeling pretty miserable, functioning in a kind of weepy, distracted way. The kids didn't know from beans, thank God! And Arthur was his usual non-communicative self.

"Then—around my birthday—Larry called me up. 'I'm moving out of my house,' he said, 'I got an apartment.' I felt that was a commitment to me and I wanted to respond in kind. I felt nervous and excited and that this was the time to tell my husband. I was ready. I had a man to go to.

"Arthur moved out. I knew he would. I had figured it out correctly. And I felt relieved. It was over. Finished. Ended.

"I realize now that I took a lover because that was the one way I could get out of my marriage. I took a lover as a catalyst to get rid of my husband. I didn't find a lover to have a fling. It was my way of telling my husband, 'Out!' To show him I had done the one thing I knew he couldn't tolerate.

"We sat it out for 18 months, Larry and I. Then, after I got the divorce, everything began to turn sour.

"Ironic, isn't it? Here I was—finally free—and Larry, too. He was out of his house. But he began to say things like, 'Gee, I don't know if I should renew my lease.' We talked about marriage, sure. But I could feel the vacillation set in. He even went to a psychologist. He couldn't let go of his wife and kids. And he couldn't grab on to me.

68

"He began to come over every night, turn on the TV, and flip dials. His indecision was irritating me. Everything was still fine in bed, but the wavering about his family was driving me nuts. He'd spend a lot of time with his daughters. He still cut the grass at their house. He even ran over during a snowstorm to dig them out. He remained tied to his family. I felt left out. Even if he wasn't sleeping with his wife, he was still part of that family emotionally. I resented it. I wanted his attentions to be focused on me. Maybe I felt a little jealous. I was hoping Larry could give me what I didn't find in my marriage.

"Then Larry started smoking and that really annoyed me, because one of my kids is allergic and would wind up in a coughing fit. He was turning into a husband! And I began to realize that having a lover while I was married was a kind of security for me. It helped me break the marriage. You see it's hard to walk out when you don't have anything to walk into. Being alone really frightened me. But knowing there was a man waiting and I wouldn't be alone—well, that made it possible.

"It was wonderful while it lasted. No regrets. But I'm smarter now, stronger, too. And I recognize that all the anger and hostility over my husband laid the groundwork. Maybe I was the cheater— the *official* cheater—but when you get right down to it, *I* was the one who was cheated.

"Maybe I'm too demanding, I don't know. I'm a lot like my father. He was 44 when I was born. Autocratic, teutonic, extremely demanding. Nothing I did was good enough. My mother felt that way too. That's probably why I married young. I had to get out. I remember my brother would bring home one A, one lousy A, and he'd get fifty cents. But when I got straight A's, I got nothing. They expected perfection. Maybe I expected it, too, from my husband and my marriage. And later my lover, too.

"I can see now that I was saying to Larry, 'Fill the void.' I was so angry at Arthur I wanted to strike back. Also, I'd run into a number of women who could look at the sex act as pure physical release. Call up a man when they were in the mood without feeling guilt. Well, I couldn't. But I saw younger women putting their needs first.

"Even while the affair was in full bloom, I felt unclean. I couldn't stand it. I would douche between my husband and my lover.

Having It Both Ways

Emotionally, I could wear a number of hats, but sexually I found sleeping with two men disturbing.

"I think you need a certain kind of ability to pull it off, to have a lover and a husband at the same time. A special talent maybe for having it both ways."

❀ ❀ ❀

Despite appearances to the contrary, there is never only *one* reason for infidelity, just as there is never only one problem in a family spat. Old wounds and long-forgotten insults are usually dragged out to buttress the case. We may say, "I won't invite Cousin Marian to the wedding because she didn't come to my birthday party." But the more powerful, overriding reason is that we're still furious because she refused to take care of the dog when we went on vacation. In every affair hostility is present in some degree. For Ada it was the chief cause: a chronic hostility fed by anger and resentment.

Other wives, too, confirm the power of hostility to push them into an affair, and to reduce their guilt.

Hostility turns to outright revenge when a wife discovers her husband is having an affair. Recent findings suggest that one out of two husbands have cheated.[*] Getting even is a powerful force. Infidelity can plunge a wife into an affair of her own.

Zalma, 41, a successful buyer for a large Dallas department store, traveled extensively.

"I made two buying trips a year to Europe. Plenty of times, men would come up to me—in airports, hotels, telephone booths. But I always turned them down. I felt kind of invulnerable because it was the farthest thing from my mind.

"Then one trip I came home a day early and found my husband in bed with another woman. Right there in my own house, in my own bed. I was furious. Hurt. I felt betrayed. Here I was being 'good' all those years while he was fooling around behind my back. What a chump, what a damn fool I was.

"I pretended to get over it, to forgive him. But in my heart I planned to get even. A one-night stand wouldn't even the score

---

[*] According to Mary Ann Bartusis' book, *Every Other Man*. However, Shere Hite's book, *The Hite Report on Male Sexuality*, puts the figure closer to three out of four.

70

because it would be too easy. Instead, I picked out his best friend to seduce. Let me tell you something. It's true: Revenge tastes very sweet.

"Call it a 'grudge fuck,' I don't care. I'm glad I did it and I continue to have affairs. That first time freed me. But now I do it for my own pleasure. I've developed a taste for variety."

Other women report similar stories. Of all the issues that cause anguish in a marriage—money, in-laws, insensitivity, alcoholism, insult or abuse—nothing seems to equal the pain of learning about a husband's affair.

"I thought it couldn't happen to us," one woman strained to hold back her tears. "Not us. I was a minister's wife. We were finishing dinner and he said he still loved me, but he was having an affair. 'With whom?' I choked. He just shook his head quietly. 'Why? What did I do wrong?' I asked him. But he only continued to shake his head and said he could make me no promises.

"I felt humiliated. I thought of doing crazy things. Of getting up on the pulpit and screaming out what he did to me. Of taking a hammer and beating him over the head so he'd know how the pain and the hurt feels. I tormented myself with questions: Did I neglect him? How long has he been cheating on me? Does the whole congregation know? I felt betrayed. Maybe I was too trusting. After all, he was a man, wasn't he?

"No matter how hard I tried to forgive and forget—it got worse. He had broken the trust. For fourteen years I was the minister's wife, so straight and narrow. And this is what I got.

"There was a nice man in the parish who seemed to like me. Widowed, quiet, a decent sort. Always hung around after the others left. So I picked him out to help me heal the scar. And he's been my lover for three years. My husband doesn't know anything. I live a double life. I have a husband and a lover, too."

Some wives seem to be able to handle a husband's affair. If it was merely a "passing fling," they are more likely to forgive it. Their anger and pain eventually subside and they may even address themselves to the problems that are damaging their relationship.

Other wives remain inconsolable. The wound is too sharp, the psychic injury too painful. The affair marks the end of trust between the couple and bleeds the marriage to death.

"I knew I could never live comfortably with him again. There was such hate in me. I didn't want him to touch me. I knew I'd never be able to forgive him. The only way out was divorce. In the meantime, to cope with the loss of my self-esteem, I found a man.

"I have to admit I am very interested in sex. I have a strong sex drive. And since I wouldn't sleep with my husband anymore, I started a little affair to rescue me from the blues. It was a lot easier than I expected. The first time I did it to retaliate for my humiliation. But once I got past that, I discovered that a woman who lives her whole life with one man is a fool. A new man is powerful medicine. As you can see, I managed to recover."

On first confronting a husband's infidelity, almost every wife reacts the same way.

"I wanted to throw myself off the nearest bridge."

"First you want to kill yourself. Then you feel like killing him."

"The bastard. I'll fix him!"

But underneath all their bravado there is still the constant fear that without a man they cannot survive. So they remain with their husbands despite their discomfort.

However, wives who forgive an occasional fling are less likely to forgive a long-term affair. That is the ultimate humiliation.

"It's not only the sex part. That part is bad, sure. But it's the intimacy my husband and the woman shared over the years. *That* bothers me most—the emotional betrayal. He was *my* husband all those years. And he had another woman all that time. A secret lover who shared his life. That he was close to someone else for so long, *that's* the part that hurts the most."

Husbands and wives may fight over children, argue over money, or quarrel over in-laws. They may shout hurtful things to each other in moments of rage, tear up love letters, hurl a wedding ring across a room, even throw a punch at the spouse. But nothing, absolutely nothing, incurs more hostility than discovering the spouse's infidelity.

Having once crossed the line, the title of faithful wife—which they defended over the years—becomes an empty one. Additional affairs may seem less traumatic. Perhaps it's like the loss of virginity. One sexual encounter and you lose the title. Then, having lost it, what does it matter? Although the first taste of "forbidden fruit" may have been motivated by hostility or revenge, it can awaken a taste for variety. Having lovers can become a way of life.

An affair can infuse a woman with energy. Many women with lovers describe themselves as "high energy" people. Hostility contained for years can lead to incessant fatigue and other physical ailments. Physicians see many women in their offices who complain of exhaustion. The effort required to hold their hostility within socially acceptable bounds drains and depresses them. Often the energy expended in taking no action is far greater than the energy used in coming to a decision and acting on it. When a woman is finally propelled by her anger to take a lover, an immense release of tension can occur.

That new energy may intensify a woman's responses to her lover, or guilt and fear over this newly released passion may rein her in.

Whether she chooses an affair or fidelity, hostility is certainly a motivation that ignites a woman.

5

Ego: Fran

WHAT DO WE get back when we look into the mirror? Do we smile back and wink impishly at that reflection—our ego inflated? Or do we mutter "Dammit! Another gray hair, another line," and quickly turn away? We face the mirror many times a day. It reports our appearance, perhaps even our state of health.

The mirror tells us how we *look* at a given moment. But it can't tell us how smart we are, how talented, how courageous, how successful, or what kind of a person we are. It reflects how we appear to others. And sometimes it lies.

A 46-year-old successful hospital administrator recalls her first junior high school dance.

"When I left for the dance, I was feeling terrific. I looked in the hall mirror and loved what I saw. My mother let me wear her pearls and I felt like a princess in my new dress. I twirled around and let the skirt fly. I was nervous, sure—but thirteen is nothing if it isn't excitement and expectation. I was Judy Garland, trembling on the inside, but gorgeous on the outside. And the hall mirror confirmed it. All the boys were going to fight over me.

"But the moment I stepped inside the gymnasium, my heart sank. I wanted to fall in a hole and disappear. Everyone was wearing skirts and sweaters. I was overdressed, completely wrong.

Having It Both Ways

Everyone stared at me, and a few of the girls giggled. I wanted to die, to tear off my mother's pearls and run. Why didn't the mirror tell me I was ridiculous—that kids in the new school don't dress up?

"I was so destroyed, it took me all of seventh and eighth grades to put that humiliation behind me and feel okay about myself again. What really saved me and repaired my ego was that in ninth grade I went to a regional high school, so I started out with a fresh image."

Besides the evidence of the mirror, we derive our ego from all the other people who react to us: parents, teachers, authority figures, pastors, mentors, brothers and sisters, peers, bosses, classmates. How they perceive us defines our strengths and weaknesses. Their estimate tells us how to judge ourselves and is a barometer of our worth. Her mother's pearls were beautiful in the mirror. Until she stepped inside the gym and was humiliated by stares and giggles.

The ego is built upon many reflections of many mirrors. A pretty young sales manager for a large department store told me about an early job experience. She had just done a "major floor move" for her department. It was a taxing day of rearranging merchandise, unpacking new arrivals, and repositioning displays. She was pleased with the result and expected generous praise from her new division head whom she wanted to impress.

"I nearly killed myself that day. Came in early and had the whole department shipshape for her arrival. But the moment she walked into my department, I knew I was in trouble. Her face was pinched and she didn't crack a smile. She brushed me aside like an ant, she said everything was wrong, everything looked terrible. The displays were in the wrong place, the traffic pattern was too tight, and the lead merchandise was too congested. She absolutely destroyed my confidence and she made me move everything back her way. What a blow to my ego!"

It takes a strong ego to overpower the negative messages we get from people everyday. However, positive feedback can do wonders, can inspire and feed the ego.

"I always dreamed of becoming an actress. I wanted to be a comedienne, a song and dance girl, but I was too embarrassed to ever express those dreams. Other kids were getting the leads in the school plays, so I figured I couldn't be that hot or some teacher would have noticed me.

"Then one day we were all gathered at my Aunt Joyce's house for Thanksgiving dinner. I was about fourteen and I was horsing around with my cousin Roberta. I put on a hat and took my grandfather's cane, and we did a little number together. Well the family went crazy, applauding and screaming with delight. Then my aunt said: 'You're talented, Dede. You're going to be famous. You're going to be a star.'

"From that moment on, I took myself seriously. I studied acting and took dance classes. I figured if Aunt Joyce saw it in me—she's a smart lady—I must be good. So far, no Broadway leads, but things are looking up. I did two TV commercials and I've got a small part in an Off Broadway play."

In both cases, an authority figure—a boss and an aunt—influenced the women's views of themselves.

As we become sexual persons, it is the opposite sex who wield the most power to set us up or knock us down. Women, especially, rely on men to define their worth. Their husband or lover informs them how valuable they are. Men, too, are judged by how they attract women. But they achieve ego stroking through many other outlets. Their careers and their salaries have always defined them. Men are what they do, what they own, what their net worth adds up to.

Until the 1940s, a woman's status was acquired through her husband's status. The doctor's wife ranked higher than the bartender's wife. Housewives ranked at the bottom of the heap. Without pay, their job of wiping children's noses, swabbing toilet bowls, and preparing meals conferred no status, power, or identity. Clean dishes got dirty again and fresh laundry got soiled.

In the 1960s, along with many other changes, housewives were euphemistically retitled "homemakers," but the change in title conferred little gain in status. Even volunteer work was no longer considered "real work." Ladies devoted to worthy causes soon defected for paid jobs. The 1970s saw the rise of the two-check family as women sought money and sometimes status outside the home:

"The only way for a woman, as for a man, to find herself, to know herself as a person is by creative work of her own," declares Sheila M. Rothman, author of *Woman's Proper Place.*° "Without work, a woman has no status, no identity."

As long as women's primary source of identity was as somebody's wife, the best way to gain status was by "marrying up." The maid who married a Rockefeller received immediate recognition. It was the Cinderella fairy tale come true.

With more than half of today's women in the work force, many of these attitudes have shifted. Women are pilots, truck drivers, nuclear scientists, bankers, publishers, soldiers—anything they want to be. And they, too, are defined by their work.

However, old values die hard. Women are still paid less than men. For many women—particularly those over 40—it is still their man's eye that establishes their sense of personal worth. The advertisers lean on that insecurity and send out subliminal messages that say: "You're exactly what your man thinks you are." If he smiles, you're pretty. If he promotes you on the job, you're smart. If he sleeps with you, you're sexy.

Do women still dress to please men?

A well-known high-fashion magazine that dictates what will be worn by chic women in every upcoming season advises: "Catch his eye." "Delight him with the new look in knits." "Seduce him with sensual stripes." The emphasis is on him, his approval, his reaction. But newer magazines, more oriented toward younger working women, take a different tack. "Express yourself with the look of success." "Celebrate your promotion with a new dress." "Reward yourself with a holiday in Spain." Here the emphasis is not on him, but her, the woman, how she feels and how she looks.

"I dress to please my husband," a young mother of twins says: "I slop around in jeans all day because the kids mess me up. But at five o'clock I clean up so my husband comes home to a good-looking gal. Of course, I dress to please him!"

"I dress to please me," a newly married gynecologist said. "When I get out of my white coat, I want comfort, something that lets me move and makes me feel good. Of course I want to look attractive

° Pages 228-29.

78

and please my husband. But I know what looks good on me better than he does because I know me longer," she grins.

Another woman, a top executive in a Burbank, California, movie studio told me: "I make six figures and I earn it. But I still dress to please men. I'm very aware of who holds the power in this business and I'm very careful about the impression I make. Women are new in production companies. I want to look businesslike so men take me seriously. But I don't want to be another man in the grey flannel suit. I let them know I'm a woman. I wear attractive feminine clothes, but no plunging necklines, nothing overtly sexual. In the working world, men's approval still counts. Don't you forget it."

Are women who need the approval of men insecure? Are those who seek men's admiration vain or more vulnerable to the flattery of another man?

"I never would have looked at Eddie if my husband had given me some attention," a 29-year-old legal stenographer explained. "He's always putting me down, telling me the meat is tough, the kids are fresh, the house is a mess. To get a nice word out of him is like pulling teeth. Even when I made him a birthday party, he complained I invited the wrong people. Nothing I did was ever right.

"Then Eddie came along—not the kind of guy I'd flip over, believe me. Short, a little overweight, with a receding hairline. But *sweet*, so damn sweet! He went out of his way to make me feel comfortable on the new job. Told me how nice I look. Well, I *am* a neat person. I keep a nice home, and I do my best. But my husband doesn't appreciate it.

"Eddie noticed me and my work from the first day. He made me feel good. When I squawked about my desk, he had a new one brought in and a divider put up for privacy. Look, he's my boss— he doesn't have to cater to me. But he was so sweet, so appreciative, I began to feel good with him around. He liked to kid me and he made me laugh. So when he invited me out for a drink, I said yes—a kind of thank you for his niceness to me. And that's how the affair began.

"When I confided in my girlfriend who works across the hall, she

was floored. 'Sheila!' she said, 'the man's over fifty, a grandfather—
what the hell are you fooling around with him for? Your husband's
got it all over him.' A lot she knows. I told her Eddie makes me feel
good about myself. When I'm with him I feel pretty and smart and
sexy. And right away, she understood. She just nodded her head
real slowly and said, 'Yeah, yeah. I know what you mean.'"

Married women know the power their husbands have to inflate
or deflate their ego. For many, just being married is a statement to
the world that says: "See, I have a husband, a man who cares about
me. I rate." In Chapter 3, Ellen was terrified of losing her husband,
and viewed it as an assault on her ego. She was willing to accept her
husband's affair as long as he wouldn't break up the marriage.

Uta West, author of *If Love Is the Question, What Is the
Answer?*, says Colette, the celebrated French writer, "well into her
fifties, accepting her final lover, commented that she could not
forego the vanity of living under someone else's gaze."[*] West feels
this is not merely vanity. "Living under someone else's gaze makes
us feel real, makes us feel alive—it keeps us from falling off the
edge, from slipping into the void."[†]

We need stroking for our egos to grow and flourish. But women
who are wholly dependent on men for their stroking may have
poor or underdeveloped egos.[‡]

Some people have egos strong enough to withstand assault,
while others suffer over the smallest expressions of disfavor. Many
psychotherapists insist insecurities and poor egos can be traced
directly back to parents who undermined their children with
impossible demands and steady disapproval. "You're not as pretty
as your sister, dear. But maybe you can be smarter and work harder
and get ahead, too." This can cause enormous damage to the ego.
Forever after—the theory goes—those people strive conscien-
tiously to gain approval. Often such women marry men who are as

[*] Page 139.

[†] Carolyn G. Heilbrun's opinion of Colette differs: "Her vantage never became man's,
where women perceive themselves through the eyes of male desire." Quoted in "Hers," *The
New York Times*, February 5, 1981.

[‡] *The Cinderella Complex*, by Colette Dowling, deals with women's hidden fear of
independence. Many women—even successful ones with happy homes—fear they couldn't
make it without a man. Like Donna, they want to be rescued, and taken care of.

demanding and disapproving as their parents. Ada, in Chapter 4, married a man as critical as her father. Donna's parents also were cold to her; her father wasn't around and her mother never held her. The husband she chose continued to chip away at her sense of self, and she came to feel that she was simply a convenience to clean his house and raise his children. Even with her lover, Donna felt insecure.

Women like Donna don't ask for anything because they feel worthless. Despite all their earnest efforts and hard work, there is something ticking away inside their heads predicting defeat, saying: "You'll never amount to much. You don't measure up." Often they go through life proving that estimate is right. They can't return a damaged piece of merchandise to a department store or end a long, time-wasting phone conversation. They are unable to ask for what is rightfully theirs. Because they don't think they are worth it they say, "It isn't worth the argument." Their top priority is to always appear "nice."

Women, especially, have been programmed to be "nice." Quite a few extramarital liaisons are based on friendly approval more than sex. They include a low-pressure sexual arrangement where one partner gives pleasure and the other receives. In such an inequitable arrangement, where the woman is rarely the receiver, a woman may say about orgasm: "Why is everybody making such a big fuss over it? It's no big deal." Dr. Irene Kassorla, author of *Nice Girls Do*, says, "Even as adults it is difficult to behave sensually, because the little child inside each of us still fears that the censoring parent will suddenly emerge to criticize and punish. . . . The amount of guilt, self-hate, and self-deprecation we've stored in our subconscious affects the degree of sensuality we can tolerate as adults."

Many married women who have faked orgasm for years fail to ask for sexual satisfaction because they feel, "It's not worth it." What they really mean is: "I'm not worth it."

The ego exerts tremendous force over what we are, what we expect, and what we receive. A successful florist, owner of a thriving nursery, showers praise on her parents for their steady encouragement: "My parents always told me I was the prettiest, the smartest, the most talented kid in town. That I could be any damn thing I pleased, if only I had guts. They said failure was nothing to be ashamed of—the shame was in not trying. So I tried to be an actress and I failed. Then I tried to be a writer and that didn't pan out either. So I tried again with plants, which I love. I gave it my best shot and . . . well, look! I'm a success." She makes a sweeping gesture toward two 50-foot greenhouses. "I guess they were right," she glowed.

❂   ❂   ❂

Fran is a bright 40-year-old speech therapist whose ambition to move up in her profession pressed her into earning a Ph.D. To hasten her advancement and insure her success, she also began an affair with the provost of her university. "I slept with my boss to get a promotion, to move up. Then I fell in love with him and we've been lovers for seven years."

She told me this on the phone, and she agreed to meet me in Boston.

Like Fran, some women—both married and single—sleep with their boss to gain favors. In the scramble to get ahead, they may use "Sleeping Up" as a replacement for "Marrying Up," the device of the fifties.

Most working women don't employ sex to get a better deal. They reject it as an unacceptable *modus operandi,* perhaps because they are women with a positive sense of their own worth, who would rather rely on accomplishment and hard work. They choose not to use what the underground calls "pussy power."

Feminists say "Sleeping Up" is anathema to the women's movement. It invites dependency on men. However, a few women like Fran still make the decision to sleep with the man in power.

How prevalent is "Sleeping Up"? I discussed this with the executive editor of a hip New York women's magazine; astonishingly, she denied its existence. "I don't know one woman, not one, who's ever slept with her boss, and I've been in publishing for twelve years." An attractive literary agent disagreed: "Of course it happens. I deal with authors and publishers and movie producers all the time. There are always women who cozy up to the man in power." The phenomenon of the casting couch for actresses seeking a good part has invaded many fields. A personnel manager of a large, New Jersey based insurance company told me, "Next to absenteeism due to drinking, our biggest problem is inter-office romances. We have to shift people sometimes because of fooling around."

The academic world is no exception. Fran deliberately made the decision to sleep with the provost soon after she met him.

I flew to Boston to talk with her.

"Come up," she said, "but not to the house, my daughter's home sick with a sore throat. And not to the university because students are always popping into my office."

We agreed to meet for lunch at a Ramada Inn. I took a cab from Logan Airport.

She was waiting for me at the bar, sipping a glass of wine. She was an attractive woman with straight shiny chestnut hair, expressive hazel eyes, and the effects of adolescent acne still noticeable on her cheeks and chin. A youthful 40, little makeup, and a big, warm smile. "I'm starved," she said, "Can we go to the salad bar and *then* talk? If I fill up on salad, I'll eat less."

It was 1:15 when we started, and the restaurant was noisy with diners. When we looked up again, it was 4:10, we were the only ones left.

"I first saw Charles at a faculty meeting. He was the new provost of the university, about 55, with a shock of white hair, and very attractive. Our relationship was purely professional, of course. I was 33, married with three little girls, and he was married, too, with grown kids. I liked him immediately. I liked his sense of humor. When I made a joke, he appreciated it.

"It was clear thinking on my part to maneuver us into an affair. I was a part-time faculty member then, and I was interested in obtaining a full-time position. I knew it would be hard to move up. I didn't have my Ph.D. yet, though I was working toward it. But there were a lot of people ahead of me in line. So I definitely considered that sleeping with him would help me and benefit my career. I had had a lover before, when I was 28. I flirted, I laughed at his jokes, and I hung around 'til the meeting was over. I also sent out signals.

83

"The next day he phoned and we went out for a drink. I was very excited, maybe because he was the provost. Also because he was an older man. We pretended we were meeting to talk about curriculum changes, but we were both aware of each other's interest. The next day, he invited me to lunch and I was even more charmed. He has the same kind of humor I have. Dry, very dry. He enjoyed every remark I tossed at him. He appreciated my jokes and caught on right away.

"The third time we went to bed.

"I was terribly nervous. Really terrified. It had been a long time, maybe five years, since my first lover. My heart was pounding. He seemed very relaxed, and I liked that he didn't jump me the minute the motel door closed. We had a drink, we talked, we joked, and I liked his sensitivity.

"My husband had no sensitivity to my feelings. He never noticed my boredom with him or the little affair I had when I was 28. See, my husband doesn't really know me. I married him at 20, he was 22, just out of college. At the last minute I remember saying to a friend, 'I have my doubts about this marriage.' But she said, 'Oh, I did, too, everyone does.' I was in too deep. The invitations were already out and my parents liked him very much, so I married him. He had a good education. He would be a good provider, and he came from a nice family. They were right about all that. We had no interests in common. There was nothing to talk about, and even our sex life was dull. My husband was very immature, very inexperienced, so I would be the one to initiate sex. When I felt it was time, I would go upstairs early—it was a signal—and I controlled the frequency. He didn't complain. It was *wham-bam, thank you, ma'am.* I never discussed sex with him. He was no experimenter, we just did it.

"I wasn't happy, but I didn't talk about it to anyone, not even my sister. There was no one to talk to. My father was not the kind of person I would talk to. He was a hard-working man, just a father, no closeness. And my mother—she wouldn't understand my feelings because we fought a lot. There was no closeness with my parents. I relied mostly on friends. I still do. In the beginning, I didn't tell anybody my dissatisfactions. I figured this is what most marriages are like. Accept it.

"I wanted another man, and after three kids and eight years, I had a brief affair.

"When Charles came along, I responded to him on two levels: as a man and as a mentor. A boss who could get me what I wanted. I knew if I had his ear, I'd be better appreciated. Part-timers rarely get pushed ahead to full time without a contact to pave the way. I didn't know a soul to help me. What better contact than the provost? It was like finding a Sugar Daddy. Oh yes, I thought it all out. I planned it. He was my Sugar Daddy. He plied me with gifts—presents, perfume, bracelets. I could have bought those things myself, but I wanted to see if he would do it. But then I fell in love with him.

"Why did I choose Charles—a man so much older? I wanted the job, sure. But I also wanted a mentor: somebody to tell me what to do. I like mean men. And in some ways, Charles is mean. He's demanding, he's jealous, he's quick to anger. So I have conflicting feelings.

"Right from the start, the chemistry was good. Although he's 22 years older than me, I never think of him in terms of age. Maybe the older he gets the more vulnerable he'll be. I see it happening already—my seven-year itch setting in. He sees me as young and girlish and terribly attractive to other men. And I like that. All that admiration and devotion give me power. But he's also very jealous, very quick to anger, and totally unpredictable. So he continues to surprise me. I mean if we go to a restaurant and we're seated next to the fire exit, he can become very rude and quick-tempered. Or sometimes he'll just accept it, so I never know.

"He's observant of everything I do. He watches me and he'll confront me about something I said offhandedly and want to discuss it. He's a fascinating man. Articles in the newspaper that pass me by will interest him. He's very intelligent, informed on so many subjects. He can talk about hot tubs and white-water canoeing, bestsellers, and how to make French pastry.

"Maybe it's his past that excites me. He's not an ivory tower academic. I hate to tell you this, but he has a notorious past. He was an M.D. whose license was revoked. Almost went to jail, which I won't go into. He was also the owner of an ice skating rink. For a while he was an actor, then he bought a supper club. Finally at the age of 55 he got his doctorate in education and moved into the provost's position. It's a colorful background and he is full of anecdotes and very open with me.

"We are not just lovers, we're soul mates. We see each other every day. We work out our schedules to share a minute together or a leisurely lunch. We talk all the time on the telephone or we'll meet for ten minutes over a drink. Since he's the provost, we meet surreptitiously so no one at the university will put two and two together. And for seven years they haven't. My husband has no idea either. As a matter of fact, we socialize. We wanted to see more of each other on weekends, so he and his wife and my husband and I go out as couples for dinner or theater. We take every opportunity to be together.

"Sometimes I say who needs this?—all the phone calls and the work and pressures to be with him. Sometimes I can't break an appointment, and once—it was our closest call—we had to make a beeline for the bathroom when some colleagues from the university came into the restaurant. Sometimes I feel seven years is too long, that's what I mean by the seven-year itch. It's like a marriage because you have a responsibility and you don't want to hurt that person's feelings. We've been through a lot together. In a way he's like a husband.

"But then I remember all the nice things Charles has done for me and I feel a responsibility. I love him but I'm at a point where I want to get rid of responsibilities. I'm tired of satisfying other people— my husband, my parents, my children. I want to be responsible for myself, no one else. Charles understands that. He's very good to me, he's very attached to me. And he's very jealous.

"We broke up once over that. If anybody makes a comment about how sexy or attractive I am, he'll infer that I've made advances to that person. He accused me of being unfaithful to him. I was once. And he's never forgiven me for it. He had me followed and he caught me and he set up ground rules that I must never never be alone with a man again. I accepted it because I wanted him back. He still checks up on me. He's very suspicious, easy to anger, moody.

"But how could I live without him? I have such a good time when

I'm with him. Other times I feel, 'Look, I'm forty—time is fleeting.' A long affair can turn into a marriage and become a burden, see? I should be experiencing things before it's too late.

"Naturally, I don't want my husband to find out. I don't want to hurt my children either. I care about my husband. We've grown up together. I care about his mother and his father and his nieces and nephews. Everyone thinks I'm the perfect wife. And I want my children to feel secure."

As the waitress refills our water glasses, she orders a chocolate eclair, explaining that chocolate is her downfall. "I'll try to feel guilty about it later," she grins impishly.

"Any married woman who has an affair is risking the end of the marriage. I know that. So it depends on how important the marriage is. In my case, it's very important, I wouldn't hurt my children for anything.

"Sometimes I think I'm cocky because I haven't been caught in so many years. It's a wonder to me. But I'm a very good actress and I know how to lie. I've even gone off on weekends with Charles. I say it's a conference, a professional meeting. We've done that a number of times. But I'm careful. We never meet nights, mostly during the day. It's easy for me. My husband has a long commute to his office and I know his hours.

"Lately, my devotion to my home and family has been replaced by other priorities. I'm changing, I'm feeling that *I'm* important and I should fulfill myself. Charles has taught me that. There's nothing sinful in fulfilling yourself. You're entitled to pleasure if it doesn't hurt others.

"Charles has made my marriage more bearable. If it wasn't him, there would be others. Having an affair is a method of letting off steam. Because my children come first, I've got to stay with the marriage. A lover makes it bearable."

She leans forward to light a cigarette.

"Charles is a fantastic lover. He taught me about oral sex and other ways to enhance sexual pleasure. I'm excited by Charles intellectually, too, and that makes the physical part more exciting. I don't know how I'd get along without him. I'd miss him so much. It's not just good sex, it's the whole relationship.

"I've had great sex though, without any emotional relationship. Yes, that's true. Before Charles I learned I could have a sexual encounter and be unemotional about it. Casual sex, sex without love, works for me, too. It surprises me, but I can do it.

"But I can't have sex with a dummy. He has to be a man of influence and power. That turns me on.

"With Charles it was a slow-developing thing. The sex was good from the start. But there was conversation and touching even before we got undressed. I don't like a man who's too hungry. I know he's going to be lousy in bed and give me a rush job. With Charles it's good because it goes on for a long time. There's foreplay and during play and lots of conversation afterward. I don't like a man who can't talk. And of course, the fact that the affair is forbidden makes it even better. Maybe that's why I quarrel with Charles and cheated on him—to keep the excitement high.

"Marriages are bound to get stale. How many happily married couples do *you* know?"

She asks me this, but it's a rhetorical question

"I know a lot of married couples, and they're all bored and unhappy. People grow. Their needs change. A woman can love her husband, have a tender, warm feeling for him, and still have a lover. I love Charles. But I also feel a sense of responsibility and loyalty to my husband. Is that crazy? I think a woman *can* have it both ways. I have. And I intend to go on that way.

"Maybe wives who take lovers are really women with a poor self image. I often wonder about that myself. Why should sexual encounters with men mean so much to me? What do I have to prove? I have an identity. I have a doctorate. I have a very important job. I'll probably be department head next semester. Still . . . having men find me attractive is very important to me. I have lots of friends who admire me, but still I need a man. I must have a poor self image, otherwise why would I need them? Objectively, I say look at all I've achieved. But it doesn't satisfy me. It's not enough. Nothing's enough. I want more.

88

"When I look in the mirror, I see a woman who's aging. I'm panicky about aging, I always have been. I'm 40, nearly over the hill. It frightens me. What'll happen when I lose my dynamism, my sexual powers? What happens when men no longer find me attractive? For me it would be hard to adjust. It would depress me terribly. Men's admiration and attraction are very important.

"As a matter of fact, if I'm at a party and I feel there's no man there who is attracted to me, the party is a dud. Having a man is what matters. We define ourselves in terms of how men feel about us. It shouldn't matter, but it does. Even a husband and a lover— *that's* not enough. It still feels great when a new man is attracted to me. But that's not enough either.

"I'm supercritical of myself, very cynical. Take the doctorate. What is it? Just a test of perseverance. What does it prove? Only that I have more perseverance than somebody else. Am I intelligent? I've seen people more intelligent. Am I attractive? I've seen people more attractive. What have I achieved professionally? Not enough."

She smiles at me, and tips her head in a little shrug.

"Maybe my expectations are too high, higher than I can achieve. Maybe that's why I'm dissatisfied. I like to have a goal, something to strive for. I'm only happy when I'm looking forward to something.

"But lately nothing excites me. A long-term lover becomes a responsibility. Like a husband. I talk to other women—women I trust because they're having affairs, too. They say the same thing. There's a network of women—I have four friends who support each other. Women who have husbands and lovers. We need supportive friends to cover up for us. We tell each other our feelings. We listen. We don't judge.

"If I had it to do over, I'd wait until I was 25 or 30 to get married and I wouldn't have children right away. I should have explored more, I'm a restless type. I should have had more lovers, but of shorter duration. Charles embellishes my life. He enriches my life, no regrets there. I've learned a lot from him about myself—most of all that I'm wonderful, I'm special. He affirms my value.

"Sometimes I think of ending the affair. But then, I'd probably start all over and find another lover, that's what I'd do. I'd be miserable without a lover. When I think of myself at 50 or 60, I think what will happen to me when the sexual part is over and men aren't interested any more?"

She pushes her coffee cup back and sighs at such a bleak future.

"What would I do without a man to tell me I'm wonderful?"

❂ ❂ ❂

The ego is a fragile thing. Fran tells us she had no closeness with her father. She fought with her mother and could not communicate with her sister. She learned finally to rely on friends.

While Fran is now an attractive, fashionable woman, one suspects that she may not have felt pretty as a little girl. Adolescent acne may have damaged her confidence and magnified her sense of her own defects. She was also chunky and continues to perceive herself as fat even years later.

Fran spends her life proving she is desirable to men. She enjoys flirting with and flattering men because only a man's approval can reassure her she is attractive and desirable.

The key word in understanding Fran is "insatiable." She hungers —for recognition in her field, to move up faster than the others, to gain better positions, to win greater prestige. Although she is admired and considered highly ambitious, she is actually so fiercely competitive that she must always drive on and is never at rest.

Early bouts with a fragile ego have kept Fran off-balance well into her adult life. "Nothing is enough," she repeatedly complains. She agonizes over whether her work is sufficiently appreciated. Even a small setback shakes her confidence. When a secretary had typed a report of hers incorrectly, Fran was certain it would reflect on *her*. It would be perceived as her defect. An inconsequential remark by a person of lesser status hurts her. She is, in a word, a perfectionist, who rarely allows herself to feel the pleasure of her attainments.

It seems almost inevitable then that Fran chose an older man for a lover: an older man who would be grateful for the attention of a woman young enough to be his daughter; an older lover who would inoculate her against criticism. His gifts would confirm her worth. She would look wonderful to him, he would tell her so repeatedly, and her ego would be stroked. A working woman's boss is in a powerful position to feed or starve her sense of worth. Many women spend more time with their boss than their spouse. Therefore, when the boss also becomes the lover, the impact is double-barreled. Disapproval and applause carry enormous weight when this combination comes up. Women who have affairs with their boss are usually aware of this, and utilize it to their benefit.

Fran's assessment of her chances to move up were probably accurate. As Professors Barbara H. and Howard P. Tuckman of Memphis State University conclude in a study, female part-timers *are* discriminated against. "Part-time employment rarely gives rise to a full-time career in academe."*

Status, of course, is not the only motivation. The attentions of a man in power flatter a woman.

Wanda, a furniture buyer for a Denver department store, says, "Sleeping with my boss didn't hurt my chances and did my ego a lot of good. It was easy to move in that direction. I depended on his approval, so his appreciation when my sales figures rose meant a lot to me. A boss is like a father, see? So it's a terrific ego trip to get his approval. And there's so much to talk about when you work together side by side every day.

"I figured it out like this. Monday through Saturday we sail the same ship, my boss and me. We're bound for the same destination. Why not enjoy the ride? If you like the guy and it's mutual, can it hurt to have him on your side? Talent, brains, they're all helpful. But if you want to move up badly enough, you go after it. Nothing wrong with that. What makes sexual favors a bigger deal than financial favors? Men use it all the time. You scratch my back and I'll scratch yours."

Carla, a 45-year-old business representative with a calculator company, says, "I do a lot of traveling for my company. That means being on the road, alone and away from everyone who

Academe, March 1980, page 76.

knows me. Sure, a lot of hanky-panky goes on—even among the 'happily married.' It's not whoring—it's just smart business tactics to sweeten a deal if you want to land the account. The surprising thing is that it's not just the older, long-married men who fool around. Younger guys are the worst."

Rosalind, a 34-year-old graphic artist, is often moving about selling to museums, schools, and public buildings. Would she consider an affair since the opportunities are so available to her?

"No. I could never do it. I'd feel dirty—like a prostitute selling herself. It's no loyalty to my husband—he's an ass. It's my *work* I'm selling, not sexual favors. I want to succeed because of the excellence of my work. Sure I try to look nice and give an attractive appearance. I'll even flirt because I enjoy it.

"But businessmen aren't fools, and bosses have contempt for the woman who sleeps with them. They may dole out favors in the beginning, but word gets out. It's a cheap device and I'm not talking morality. I'm talking about self worth. I don't operate in the meat market. I'm damn good at what I do, damn good! I don't muddy up my work with bedtime favors. What I'm selling is my work, not my body. If I sleep with a guy for a sale, I'll never know how good my work is and that matters to me. Work—that's what I care about.

"It's bad business to sleep with a fellow to gain an advantage. I'd be scared wondering if it's my bedtime shenanigans or my presentation he's buying. And if sex goes wrong, no matter how good my work is I'm out."

Samantha, a fund raiser for a Denver non-profit organization, agrees. "I don't mix business with pleasure. Only an insecure or incompetent woman tries it. She can't perform on her job and figures a sexual performance will rescue her. Bull! You sleep with a guy and you may get a few favors at first. But his patience will run out eventually. He's not going to look like a fool by putting an ineffective woman in a powerful position even if she is hot stuff in bed. He might buy her a few baubles to feed her ego—even take her on a trip. But he's only using her. She'll never move up if she can't cut the mustard. Women who play sex games don't move up, they move out. I'd never take that chance, even though my husband can be an awful pain and I've been tempted."

Lena Horne, in a full-page ad in *Savvy*, titled "I've Come A Long Way . . . Maybe"* talks about her background. "Strength is where I get my feelings of security," she says. "I've always had to sing for my supper. At first it was to pay my mother's bills. Then it was to pay my children's bills. Then it was to be a credit to my race. And then, of course, to my gender—to prove I was more than a Cotton Club cutie.

"Well, I'm still singing. But I'm singing for Lena now. I know what I'm all about and I don't expect everyone to love me anymore."

Valerie, a third-grade teacher married eleven years, told me how she deals with a blow to her ego. "Sure I feel down sometimes, who doesn't? When things pile up at home with the kids, and my husband is bitching, and my mother—she lives with us—is complaining, I can feel pretty sorry for myself. Poor me, I'm so unappreciated. Especially if my husband's had a hard day, too, and he comes down on me. But I don't cheat. It wouldn't make me feel better, it would make me feel worse.

"Know what I do? I treat myself to 'Valerie's Day of Pleasure.' I take a personal day off from school and I devote the whole day to *me*. Why not? I'm worth it. I go to the Mall, buy new lingerie, get my hair done, a facial maybe or a massage at the gym. I pamper myself. It makes me feel terrific. I arrive home with my ego in a better state."

For most women, having an affair is a matter of ego. But it should be said that for some women their affair is not the result of a need for flattery and assurance. Taking a lover can be an act of courage. The intimacy of a new sexual and emotional bond may bring rejection. The woman who can risk that is perhaps stronger than the one who is locked into an unhappy marriage and accepts her fate. Therefore, reaching out to another man is in some cases an affirmative and positive stance.

Perhaps the Jewish spiritual leader Hillel said it best. About 2,000 years ago—before Freud gave us the id, the ego, and the superego; before consciousness-raising groups and assertiveness training;

*September 1980, page 21.

Having It Both Ways

before rap sessions and the human potential movement—he said in
"Ethics of the Fathers,"

> If I am not for myself, who is for me?
> And being only for myself, what am I?
> And if not now, when?

6

SEX: JANE AND BETTY

MARRIED WOMEN GENERALLY don't allow themselves to fall head over heels in love—at least not at the beginning of an affair. An affair usually begins with sexual arousal. But a married woman's ties to her husband, her guilt over illicit sex, her sense of responsibility toward her children—all serve as natural restrictions.

But sex can slowly become love. A woman thinks about her lover. She begins to fantasize. To romanticize. Eventually she may abandon herself to passion. She may "fall in love."

"I love my husband," a 32-year-old decorator told me. "But I'm *in* love with another man. They're two different feelings, worlds apart."

Love. Passion. Sex. Affection. Lust. Fondness. Devotion. Adoration. So many words for the emotions couples feel toward each other. Webster's first definition of love is *a deep and tender feeling of affection*. But if you've *fallen in love*, it's not the same feeling. "Is it love or is it sex?" people wonder. The distinctions are often difficult to make.

Judging from the thousands of letters that pour into the lovelorn columns, people are constantly falling *in* and *out* of love.

"It just happened. We didn't plan it. We couldn't help ourselves,' lovers explain. "It's like the song that says that *you made me love you, though I didn't want to do it*. We were helpless."

Having It Both Ways

In addition to falling *in* and *out* of love, we also *make* love. Which means having sex. And we use a lot of colorful words for making love: screwing, laying, balling, fucking, tricking, humping, and doing it. Though more fastidious and clinical-minded people prefer the respectable words: sexual intercourse, coitus, copulation. Television, magazines, and movies (not R or X rated) like the euphemistic "sleeping together," though the amount of sleeping that accompanies sex may be negligible. The Old Testament called it "knowing a woman."

We often use the words sex and love interchangeably because they baffle us. Even the experts disagree. Havelock Ellis felt love was more important than sex. Sigmund Freud considered romantic love a sex urge that was blocked. And Theodore Reik insisted sex and love were quite different. The sexologists continue to have their say, but the popular view remains that love is a crazy, mysterious, unexplainable state which captures us against our will and comes and goes unreasonably. Despite researchers delving into the subject, measuring responses, arranging questionnaires, and assembling data, we're still in the dark. When the popular song asks: "What is this crazy thing called love?" most of us reply with a shrug: "Beats me."

But when it strikes we recognize the effects.

"It felt like someone hit me over the head with a sledge hammer," a desk clerk in a Holiday Inn told me. "I was miserable. I couldn't eat. I couldn't sleep. I was a basket case. All I could think about was Kenny, what he said, how he looked.

"It's crazy. I always wanted a man over six feet because I'm so tall. Well, he's 5'6" and he's wonderful. How did I know it was love? When I started reading poetry again, I knew it. Every love poem had a private meaning for me, like it was a personal message about *us*."

Another woman described the effect love had on her friend Roberta, whom she met each Tuesday in slimnastics class.

"I could tell absolutely when it happened to Roberta. I knew she was having an affair and it was obvious to the other women, too. Her appearance changed. She lost weight, maybe ten or fifteen pounds. Bought sexy new lingerie, wore smarter clothes and new makeup. She was dreamy and distracted. She'd show up late. And she got very quiet, hardly opened her mouth at our rap sessions. It was a dead giveaway. I knew Roberta was in love."

Besides changing one's outward appearance, falling in love jolts the personality.

"It hit me like a bolt of lightning," a 33-year-old dog trainer told me. "I have no idea how it happened. But from the moment I fell in love with Stanley, my whole personality changed. It was magic, like a supernatural force took over my personality. I felt transformed and everything turned beautiful. I started noticing things: the sky, the birds, the trees. People seemed to sparkle. I wanted to skip, not walk. I sang along with the car radio when I drove to work. Once when I was stopped for a red light, the man in the car next to me shook his head like I was nuts. I was singing my heart out. What could I tell him? I'm in love, mister, I'm in love!"

Actress Liv Ullman confesses similar feelings:

"I felt as though the clouds were not on the horizon but under my feet. How sweet it was."*

The problem of sex and love has been studied by many researchers. But it was not until Kinsey's breakthrough in 1953 that the subject of sex became part of popular literature. Books by Masters and Johnson, Comfort, Friday, Hite, Gornick, Barbach, Hunt, and others were gobbled up by a public eager to find out what had been hidden in the science closet. Women readers especially led the way, buying books by women writers: Colette, de Beauvoir, Friedan, Jong, French, Decter, Nin, Greer, Chesler, Steinem, Janeway, and others.

Private researchers investigating family life, marriage, and changing lifestyles continue to probe for answers. So does our government. The White House Conference on Families has discussed these problems and the government has allocated tens of thousands of dollars for studies of love.

The National Science Foundation, for example, gave an $84,000 grant to study love and discover the difference between passionate and compassionate love. Sound frivolous? Senator William Proxmire considered this a waste of the taxpayer's money. In a *New*

***McCall's*, February 1977, page 205.

York Times article,* he said, ". . . no one—not even the National Science Foundation—can argue that falling in love is a science." Dr. Elaine Walster, the researcher who was the object of Senator Proxmire's Golden Fleece Award, defended her study. "If there was ever an area that needed research, this is it: to find out about marriage and what's realistic, what's reasonable to expect."

What did Dr. Walster uncover? Among other things that, ". . . 6 to 30 months is the average duration of the kind of heart-stomping, I'm-about-to-faint romantic frenzy we all think of as being in love."

For some lovers, this may be viewed as *good* news. Remembering the pain of being in love they may welcome the news that passion abates in a couple of years. But for most of us—incurable romantics that we are—the 6–30-month decree is bad news. We mourn the death of passion and want it never to end.

"It was total bliss," one woman told me, "I was in heaven. But it only lasted two years. Then it was over. So short a time, then gone." Romantics lament the passing of passion, that two and a half years is all we can expect. "Affection and friendship are nice, sure," a beautician said, "but passion, ah!" Then she danced off singing: "Those were the days, my friend, I wish they'd never end, la la la la . . ."

When passion wanes, some women feel cheated. The loss of sexual passion seems to be the death of their marriage. They long for the "glorious feeling" of being *in* love, the excitement that occurs with sexual stirring. When that excitement is absent from the marriage they are tempted to reach outside.

❀   ❀   ❀

I phoned Jane while I was visiting friends out on the coast. She had heard about this book from them and said she'd be willing to talk to me.

A stunning woman in her mid-fifties, blonde, blue-eyed, 5'10", she was an altogether glamorous figure.

"Come in," she smiled as she literally swept me inside, her cool blue eyes appraising me. She wore a floor-length, royal blue caftan embroidered at the neckline with birds and slit to reveal her thighs.

* July 28, 1978.

98

The apartment was magnificently appointed. Sliding glass doors off the living room led to a private garden.

"I like beautiful things," she said. "I own the building. I'd get a better view of the ocean from the penthouse, but I can keep my eyes on things from here. Let me show you the rest of the place."

Unlike some of the other women, Jane was very much in command and aware that I was on "her" turf. She gave me a room-to-room tour, saving the bedroom for last. It was about 40 by 20 feet, done in lavenders and pinks. Center stage was a king-size canopied bed, dressed in satins and covered with pillows. A mirrored ceiling doubled its splendor.

"You could live in this bedroom for a week and never leave. Watch this." She slid the glass doors open and the Jacuzzi—and indeed the bedroom itself—became one with the outdoor garden.

We sat down around her dining room table, and she filled me in on her background. "I'm not married now. But I had two husbands. The first was going nowhere. The second was the love of my life. The Prince Charming of Cafe Society."

"Hold it, hold it," I said. "I want to get it all down on tape."

"I'll say it again for the tape," she assured me.

"I was 17 when I got married. Started out with stars in my eyes. The cottage and the picket fence. But I had a baby in nine months, and shortly after that, another baby. So I ended up a drudge. I was miserable—emotionally, financially, in every way.

"So I went to work. I took a job at night as a hatcheck girl. From there I went to cigarette girl, and soon I was running all the concessions. I didn't sleep much, but I made good money. Men seemed to like me. I was aggressive. Survival."

She taps a long fingernail on the dining room table. "Survival is the most important instinct you have. I figured a way out. In the daytime I stayed home with the babies. And I started to plan.

"At the beginning it was the money. I *had* to work. But that gave me a taste of the world. I liked what I saw. Liked being part of the mainstream of things. I saved money, bought a suitcase, lined up a taxi driver and got out. Me and the two babies. I called my father and I said, 'I'm leaving my husband.' And he said, 'It's about time.' It took me five years to get out of that rut.

Having It Both Ways

"My first husband was a mailroom clerk with no ambition. He hated every day. On his tombstone, they'll say: 'A Faithful, Dedicated Worker.' Some people are happy if they have a roof over their head. Not me. The only place we got along was in bed. Even with him, I enjoyed sex. Because I'm a sensuous woman. But I found a way out. I found a lover. That's how I did it. I sent out signals. A man knows when a woman is looking. He paid all my expenses. I was looking for a way to better my position."

She looks me squarely in the eyes. We are not more than a yard apart. She is tough. She is glamorous.

"My lover was in a better position in life to give me the things I wanted. I married him on my twenty-fourth birthday. He divorced his wife for me. He was 40. Handsome, sexy, sophisticated.

"We lived a very glamorous life. He opened doors for me to the best. A whole new lifestyle.

"I met interesting people. I traveled all over. We had two kids together. Plus my two made four. We sent the kids to the best schools. We lived in grand style. He was in show business, a producer of musical comedies. We ran a dinner club together, plus a music business and a few lucrative spin-offs. It was a wonderful life. He was a living doll, and we had a marvelous relationship.

"No, it didn't last forever. What lasts? But while it did it was heaven. People say marriage is for a lifetime. Well, that's saying I'm going to serve a lifetime sentence even if it becomes unbearable. I think it's impossible to sustain one monogamous relationship. It's not normal. Either you settle into a boring life or you compromise. For this you give up that—you say I have food on the table, a roof over my head, my children have a home—I'll stick it out. Mistake.

"I know very few happy marriages. In my whole life I only had one aunt and one uncle who remained devoted. My own parents were divorced. My father's been married several times. My mother, too.

"I disliked my mother intensely. But I adored my father. Look, biological fact does not create love. My mother was always grasping at me for love and I couldn't stand to have her touch me. I think she was jealous of my relationship with my father. He was so handsome, so virile. Women were crazy about him and he did fool around. My mother knew. Around menopause she finally went off her rocker. I support her, but I don't love her. Maybe I didn't have good role models," she laughs ruefully. "Two of my kids are divorced, too."

"My second husband was the greatest lover that ever existed. We did everything together, every sexual act you can imagine. He was a very creative person. Not only in his work, but in bed, too. He had a talent for making love.

"We did the whole bit. He liked to dress me up in black stockings and stiletto heels. We had all those costumes in wardrobe. We would never swing with other couples, no. But between the two of us we screwed every way and everywhere. We even screwed in the darkroom in the basement. Any time. Any place. It was a spontaneous thing—the moment! It never got boring. We had no sexual hang-ups, and we didn't analyze sex. We did what we wanted. We had oral sex, both ways. We had anal sex, too, which I was willing to do, but it's not my thing. We stimulated each other sexually with our fantasies. But it wasn't just physical pleasure. It was great sex because we loved each other.

"Look, I don't believe in Erica Jong's zipless fuck. The idea of fucking without any emotional attachment is bullshit. What Erica Jong has done is arouse a possibility in young, unsophisticated minds—young women who haven't really lived yet. They're not going to find it as satisfying as they think. I've had many fucks. It's a physical need—you have an itch and you scratch. Sex takes care of it temporarily because without sex there's something missing in your life. But the greatest sex is with someone you're emotionally involved with.

"When a married woman takes a lover just for sex, no matter what she says, she's risking getting involved. And that means breaking up the marriage. If you've ever had sex with love, you know the difference.

"It's true for women as well as for men. Men get involved. Without intending to, they do. They consider themselves Lotharios, they go out to screw everything that's walking. It starts as pure sex. Lust. But eventually they screw somebody they become involved with. Men carry off sex without love. But they still have the same tear-ups inside. They're just as vulnerable. I know. Take my second husband. I saw it happen. He started having an affair with me. He was still married—an eighteen-year marriage. He had no intention of marrying me. He thought I would be just one in a series. But he got involved emotionally. He fell in love. It broke up his marriage. He married me."

When I ask her how she felt about that, her eyes narrow. Clearly, she resents that question.

"I didn't *want* to break up his marriage. But I got involved, there was this terrific chemical reaction. Then the picture changed. I went after him. It's survival—you live by your wits."

Having protested, she moves away from the subject. Throughout, she never says her husband's name.

"My husband was the love of my life. He represented everything I ever wanted. Until he became ill. That's when everything changed."

She announces this almost reverently.

"He had a heart attack and became an alcoholic as a result.

"It's very rough to be married to an alcoholic. Someone destroying everything you've worked for. He couldn't face up to being ill. It was about 16 years into our marriage when the party was over. We separated just before he died. Actually he committed suicide. He killed himself.

"He checked into a hotel and bled to death. He slit his wrists. He was a hypochondriac—always on sleeping pills—a very high-strung man. A talented man. Anybody that creative and talented is high strung. It's part of the price you pay for your talent. He was threatening to swallow sleeping pills, was under psychiatric treatment by that time. You see, being ill drove him over the edge.

"To think he slit his own wrists. Here was a man who couldn't stand to cut his finger, feared illness and dying. Couldn't stand the sight of blood. And he killed himself. In the worst possible way.

102

"When he became an alcoholic, we had sex problems. When someone takes up drinking, they lose interest in sex. Contrary to what some people think, alcohol is not an aphrodisiac."

She tries to chuckle, but only a sad little *hmpf* comes out.

"That's when I started cheating on him. I was looking for some comfort. I felt guilty about it. Oh, not for religious reasons. I don't believe in organized religion. I was brought up an Episcopalian, converted to Catholicism for my first marriage, became a Presbyterian for my second marriage. I find the Jewish religion attractive. I'm not guilty about my cheating either. No. I needed the sex! What I felt guilty about was my hate feelings. I felt nasty. Guilty about having survived him. Guilty for being strong. I'm a strong woman.

"So that's when I went into my *experimental* period. Full tilt, full blast fucking. All your life you read about men on the road picking up a body to go to bed with. I decided to try it.

"I traveled a lot. Every town I went to, I found somebody. I'll tell you what I discovered."

She leans forward.

"A lot of men have sexual problems. Tremendous problems. Not only physical, emotional problems. I didn't find it so much with younger men, but my contemporaries—the over-40 crowd—terrific problems.

"I met this attorney around the swimming pool. We were both guests at the hotel, there on business. He came on strong. But in bed, my God, his penis was so small he could barely have an erection. There was nothing there. There was also this young boy who came into town—28, into music. A kid so large I couldn't enjoy making love, it was painful. This boy had tremendous self-confidence because the culture has told him he's a real man. He puts on bathing trunks and he's got it made. But it's an impediment to making good love. The size of the penis isn't important, only if it's abnormal. Most men are built the same.

"There were so many. The most unexpected men turn out to be the best lovers. Here's one for the books. An unattractive man. Short. Fat. Highly successful and very rich. He turned out to be a fantastic lover. He knew how to please a woman. Anything I wanted.

"A woman is a very sensuous creature. Her skin is sensitive, her ears are sensitive, her breasts, her nipples, every part. A lot of men want oral sex for themselves, but they don't want to perform it on a woman. This man did it all. He went down on me and it was a very enjoyable thing. The physical appearance of a person has nothing to do with good sex.

"What makes a great lover? A man who is attuned to a woman's vibes, isn't selfish. A woman is the director of sex, she can get a man to do anything for her if she handles him properly. You can be aggressive and yet be passive. You have to listen to your own body and your own feelings.

"Women got too far away from that. They lost their ability to feel themselves as persons. They were always reacting to somebody else. This guy—this great lover—homely as he was, knew all that. His money turned me on, too. I find money sexy. Very sexy."

I feel now is the right time to press a hard question: "Have you lived off men?" I ask her.

"Never! Never financially. I *worked* through both my marriages. I only took time off to have babies. I pulled my weight. And I didn't cheat until my husband became an alcoholic.

"A chemical reaction—oh, I believe in it strongly! It's a great feeling! A beautiful high! That lust, the chemistry, the mad desire for each other. Sex is the flint to get the fire going. But love—*that* intensity—you feel through your pores. When it was good with my husband we could look across a room at each other and know we'd make love that night. That was love!

"Would I marry again? I have no reason to get married. Unless someone came along that filled the bill one hundred percent. Financially, emotionally, sexually—I want it all.

"Right now I'm between lovers and I don't mind. My last lover was very very wealthy. He worshipped me. He was very good to me. But there was no chemistry. Sexually, I settled for less. Being his mistress was superior to being his wife. He was married of course—if they're not married they're usually not worth having—

but she was like a sister to him. We had wonderful times together. We'd fly to the Caribbean, Mexico, all over. We'd go to the beach, loll around the hotel with a bucket of champagne, fuss around the stores shopping. But in bed, I couldn't improve him. He was so darling, so loving. He adored me. Showered me with gifts.

"Money has always been a very important motivation for me. The sexiest man in the world could walk in here, but if I found out he was a plumber—a complete turn-off. A gorgeous hunk of man—if he was a construction worker—I couldn't work up a thing for him. Money represents power. It represents achievement. A man who hasn't achieved anything wouldn't appeal to me. I'm an achiever. Money matters.

"See all those older men with their bellies sticking out? They think they're attractive to young women. The only thing that's attractive is their money, their position. If they're old and fat and poor, they don't get a young woman. But if they're rich. . . . They kid themselves into thinking they're virile, they're sexy. But it's the money.

"Right now I'm well off. My lover died, but he always told me he was going to take care of me. Not to worry, he said. He left me 25 percent of his estate."

> She rises to indicate the interview is over and beams me one last dazzling smile. We have been sitting there for hours. My stomach rumbles, and I realize she has not offered me a cup of coffee, a cookie, a glass of water.

"And there's a new man in my life. Well, he's not *in* my life, but he's going to be. He's on the fringe. He doesn't know it yet. But *I* do!"

❖   ❖   ❖

Betty was 32 when I interviewed her, a full generation younger than Jane. However, their stories bear certain resemblances. For that reason, I've included a portion of Betty's story here—though you'll hear more about her in a later chapter. Despite the disparity in their ages, both women's backgrounds touched similar bases.

Both married young, quickly had two children, and were Catholic at the time. Both found lovers in their twenties, only a few years into the marriage. Both took for their lovers married men whom they met at work. And both convinced their lovers to leave their wives and children to marry them.

Jane and Betty took similar routes, yet they observed different scenery, heard different bird songs, and expressed different feelings about their experiences.

"At first I was sorry I told you to come all the way to Maryland. But now I'm glad. I think it's an important book you're working on."

Betty's voice on the telephone was a little girl's voice—soft and vulnerable. So I expected to see an ingenue open the front door. Instead, a sturdy young woman greeted me from behind thick tortoise shell eyeglasses. She wore a freshly pressed red cotton shirt and black slacks. Not a trace of makeup. A scrubbed, round face, blue eyes and short, blond hair. No nail polish or jewelry.

We sat at her dining room table and she promptly brought two cups of coffee from the kitchen. It was a dark mahogany, Old World room of heavy carved furniture and green brocade drapes—an anachronistic setting for a contemporary woman barely out of her twenties. Betty seemed older than 32, staid for her years.

"I was married five years when I met Jerry. Had two little kids. I got married at 20, a kid myself. I met Jerry at work. It was my first job since I got married, so I was excited and scared. My husband was an airline pilot. He was laid off, out looking for a job and we needed the money. This job came up only a mile from the house, so I answered the ad and I got it.

"Jerry was the vice president of the company. I became his secretary, so I saw him every day. A lot of men were fooling around at work, but I'd always say no. Jerry never came on to me—he was married and had children. He was very self-confident, almost too sure about everything, so I kind of disliked him. Believe me it was *not* love at first sight."

She laughs, allowing a crack in her serious demeanor. She is feeling more comfortable, warming up.

"And yet I have to admit I admired him. He had a strictly business personality. He was very independent. Cool. Almost arrogant.

"Then around the holidays, there was a Christmas party in one of the large offices. He didn't come. He was in the building, but he stayed in his office while everyone was kissing and drinking. So I went to see what he was doing. I had my coat on to leave and he said, 'Well, don't I get a Christmas kiss?' It sounds so childish, doesn't it?"

She giggles, transformed to that girl again, embarrassed, pleased, and aroused. And she grows younger, prettier, even flushed.

"I gave him a kiss. It *wasn't* a little peck. I mean we *kissed*. Then I went home. But after that kiss, everything seemed different. I was sexually aroused. I felt more mellow toward him. and he became more attentive to me.

"For one whole month after that kiss I didn't see him outside the office. Look, I was a virgin when I got married and I never slept with another man. I was a faithful wife. My husband was away a lot. But I enjoyed the time alone. And I never went out behind his back. But after that kiss, I couldn't stop thinking about Jerry. I couldn't.

"A month went by. I waited. He didn't call. I kept thinking about him. I wanted him.

"One day I came home from work. I was alone. My husband was away. And I called him. I couldn't stand it anymore.

"When can I see you?" he asked.

"Tonight."

"That night we slept together. We went to a motel room. It was like a sleazy movie. I wanted to have sex with him. He wanted me, too. There was no question about it. That was why I met him. I had a physical need to be with him. Sex. Pure sex.

"From the very first time it was good, sexually satisfying. But I felt guilty, so guilty. I didn't tell anyone. I felt too guilty.

"The funny thing is sex with my husband wasn't bad up to then, though it deteriorated fast afterward. There were things my husband wanted me to do that I didn't enjoy. They disgusted me, but I did them anyhow. I felt I loved my husband at that point so I wanted to make him happy, to please him. He was a good father to our children, a good provider. But sexually . . . the truth is he was not sensitive to my needs. And he wasn't sensitive to my feelings either. I guess I was more like a mother to him. He would say, 'Things are terrible, I don't know how we're going to get back on our feet.' And I'd have to say, 'Don't worry.' I always had to be the strong one. Well, I just got tired of being strong. I needed somebody to cry to, to lean on.

"After that first time at the motel, another month went by and we were just co-workers. I felt angry thinking maybe he had used me, got what he wanted and was playing it cool. It was a bad month for me after the first time we had sex. A month of avoiding each other's eyes, being very short with one another. I wanted him badly. It was hard. So I called him again.

"We drove 60 miles away. But that night we did *not* have sex. We just had dinner and talked. But after that night we started a real affair. We began to see each other regularly. Once a week. At a prearranged time and a prearranged place. We moved into a new relationship. We became lovers.

"Having sex with Jerry made everything else seem different. Now when I had sex with my husband, I'd just wait for it to be over. All I wanted was Jerry. It started as sex but I fell in love with him. It changed my marriage.

"I guess my motivation for taking a lover was my need to have someone care about me, just for me. The need for someone to look at me and enjoy it when I smiled, get pleasure out of seeing me happy. It was sex at first, but it grew into love. It changed just as I did. I was a little girl at 20. But now I was changing into a woman. . . .

"The first year Jerry and I were lovers I wasn't even scared about getting caught. It was fun, a fun kind of fright. An adventure. He knew a lot of prominent people so there was always the chance of running into someone. Soon I was hoping we would. Because it got to a point where I wanted him to give up his marriage.

"I couldn't take the affair, all the ramifications of it. I wanted Jerry to tell me he'd leave his wife for me. I wanted that commitment. We avoided saying we loved each other. He had two boys he was close to, but he didn't love his wife. I had two small children. So

I said: 'Okay, we'll have what we have, and we'll continue married to someone else.' I thought we could have pure sex. But then, after a short time, I realized I couldn't do that.

"I was very unhappy with the situation. Sneaking around and having a lover was being dishonest. And I was living a lie. I was also sure my husband never cheated on me—we had an honest relationship that way. My father and two brothers were happy with my marriage. I don't think much of my father as a man, but it was a blow when I told him I was leaving my husband. He told me I was making a mistake. But he wasn't thinking of me. He was thinking he'd lose his place in heaven because of my actions. Even the priest told him to leave me alone.

"Jerry and I continued meeting. But I decided I couldn't handle the affair. I wanted more. More than sex. It was more important to be able to walk down the street with Jerry than to maintain the marriage. So I told Jerry I'd stop seeing him unless he left his wife. I insisted I could not continue with the affair.

"A week went by—one awful week. Then he called. He said yes, he would leave his wife. And yes, he wanted to marry me.

"I was so happy! However, I was *not* about to leave my husband or even tell him at that point. I guess I was testing Jerry. For the year and a half we were sleeping together, I felt it was mainly sex. I had never spent a night with him. Just sex and I'd come right home. Then I discovered I wanted more. I wanted him to assure me it was more than just a sexual thing.

"But on the other side, I wasn't ready to break up my marriage. I cared deeply for my husband and I didn't want to hurt him. Absolutely not. I couldn't tell him until he got back to his job.

"At that time Jerry was living in a very affluent neighborhood— the country club set and all that. He was a top executive, making over $50,000, with 400 people under him. But I had no thoughts for the financial part. No, for me it was a romantic thing. A sexual thing.

"I waited three years before I told my husband. Three long years. It was terrible. I was exhausted. I look back on it now and it seems like it was not me—it was a different person."

She pushes her chair back to refill our coffees. I can see she is tired, but she says she only needs a break. "It's so hard to talk about after all these years. But it's important for other people to know about the feelings you have during an affair." We sip coffee and start again.

"By this time I knew I loved Jerry and he loved me. What began as pure sex had grown to love. I felt he needed me for no other reason than . . . just me. It was the greatest turn-on.

"Sex was so good with him. I could do things with him that repulsed me with my husband. I don't know why—and this is going to sound silly—but my husband was very hairy and I didn't like that. Jerry is not hairy so there were things I could do that didn't repulse me."

Betty is blushing now and I tease her that we will refer to her as Blushing Betty. She laughs easily and I know she is beginning to trust me.

"Also Jerry was so gentle, he took time with me. He didn't expect some of the things my husband forced on me.

"With my husband, I didn't know what pleased him. He was only 21 when he got married—inexperienced too. I always felt I might be doing it wrong. It was a silent kind of lovemaking. Sometimes I'd say, 'No, that doesn't feel good,' or 'Wait a second.' But he didn't pay attention. When I said I didn't like it, or it hurt, and I don't care *how* many people do it, he'd still try. Like with anal sex. I find it hurts. I would try to explain it to my husband: 'How would you like me to stick something like that up *your* rear end?' But he wouldn't understand and he'd get mad. If he couldn't climax, he would try anything, I mean kinky things I didn't like. He started to bring home dirty books, porno magazines, and he wanted me to pose for dirty pictures. I didn't like oral sex with him either. But with Jerry I do.

"Maybe I forced my husband into these kinky things. Maybe I was a factor in making him turn to them. He was desperate, trying any kind of sex to satisfy himself. I'm blaming myself because before Jerry, we had a normal sex life. Now he wanted me to dress up and do terrible things you see in porno magazines. But maybe if I were able to give him what I gave my lover, he wouldn't need them. So maybe I drove him to it.

"It went on like that for three years. I was torn.

"Then Jerry left his wife. He left *his* house, but I was still living the same life at home with my husband. Even after my husband got his job back, I didn't tell him. Something was holding me back. I didn't want to hurt my husband. I cared about what would happen to him.

"Maybe I loved them both. I believe . . . I believe . . ."

Betty lowers her voice for an inner dialogue with herself. She tilts her head to one side to consider the argument she is raising.

". . . it's possible to love more than one man. Yes, I believe that. Maybe society compels us to make a choice. But I felt: Why can't I have them both—my husband and my lover, too?

She chuckles and comes out of her musings.

"No. I'd never be willing for Jerry to love me and another woman. No, I guess it's impossible. So I don't think you can have it both ways. A woman who takes a lover eventually will divorce the husband, or get rid of the lover. Make a choice one way or the other. You can't continue with two people for long. Sure I did it for three years. But the last two were hell. I wasn't sleeping at night. I was worried about the children. Worried about my husband. Worried about what my family would think. The only happy times were when I was with Jerry, not thinking about the consequences.

"The night I told my husband—oh, it was terrible. We were down in the rec room. He had just come home from a trip. He was sitting on the couch—I can see him—and I was standing up ironing. The phone rang. It was Jerry. 'Either you tell your husband you're leaving him or it's over!' And he hung up.

"I must have turned scarlet. I put the phone down and I thought, 'I'm going to die. What do I do now?' I knew Jerry meant it. So I told my husband. I said, 'There's something I've got to tell you. I no longer love you. I've been going out with someone I care very deeply about. I don't want the marriage.'

"'What are you telling me? Can't we talk about this?' He went crazy.

"'No.'

"I was very unfair. And . . . and . . . uh, I'm going to cry. I, I . . ."

Betty breaks down. She weeps with abandon. Long aching sobs from deep inside. She lays her head down on the table and cries into her arms. When she finally lifts her head, she says very simply, "It's painful to relive it." She removes her glasses, and from inside the black slacks, she withdraws tissues and dabs at her eyes.

"The one thing I never wanted to do was hurt him. So I had to be honest. He was so, so crushed."

She cries quietly now, dabbing and sniffling.

"When he found out it was Jerry, he was furious. He said he was going to get someone, this fellow in the Mafia. It was crazy talk.

"He called me a whore and an adulteress. It was terrible. Adulteress. How can I forget? I am an adulteress—it's the word used in the Church.

"I had stopped going to the Catholic Church soon after I married because you cannot practice birth control. *Can not!* Only rhythm. Well, rhythm doesn't work. My second daughter was born almost immediately after my first. So I decided the only way to have a decent sex life was to take the pill. Then I could not continue being a good Catholic. I was brought up a very strict Catholic. And now . . . I am an adulteress. It's terrible if you're Catholic.

"I belong to the Unitarian Church now. That gives me some sense of feeling religious. No, I don't feel I've lost my place in heaven. Whether or not I believe in God anymore—I don't know. I broke from the Church He supposedly heads. But He can't help see I've tried to lead a good life and not hurt anyone. If there is a God, He won't disapprove. If there is a Good and Holy person—why should He want me to have children I can't handle? My father—well, he still has difficulty over my divorce and my marriage to Jerry."

She lowers her eyes and shrugs.

"Sometimes . . . sometimes I say to myself: Why? Why did I do this? Sometimes when I'm alone, I think I wish this had never happened. I had sex with Jerry and then I fell in love with him and married him. Sexually, it's still very good. It's different—not that passionate kind of thing you have during an affair. But it's still very good. He's still very romantic, still buys me little things and does nice things for me. But naturally, I wish I was never involved in a divorce and an affair and all that pain.

"I couldn't have it both ways. I don't think anyone can."

❉   ❉   ❉

Both Betty's and Jane's stories illustrate what we all know. Sex is a powerful motivation, inside or outside marriage.

However, despite the sexual revolution, and current liberal views, some married couples do *not* know the most elementary ABC's of sex. Betty's husband, a boy married at 21, is an example. They may be familiar with the physiology of reproduction and the biology of the sexual organs. Even fifth graders—informed by sex education classes—are acquainted with the diagrams and the correct words for the male and female parts. But some of the most basic and practical facts still escape married couples—especially long-married couples.

A married woman who takes her first lover is very concerned about her ability to please him. Knowing only her husband and perhaps a limited number of other men, she may feel insecure about aspects of her sexuality, about revisions in her birth control methods, about infection. She may consult a physician for information or reassurance. But physicians, who could be guides in these matters, are frequently incapable of discussing sexual problems. When they are consulted, instead of dispelling ignorance, they sweep the question under the rug or take a paternalistic attitude.

A 50-year-old woman said, "When I asked my gynecologist why my perfectly healthy uterus had to come out when he did the bladder surgery, he just patted my shoulder and said, 'Don't worry, honey. Leave it to me.' Well, I'm a medical technologist and I like answers. So I persisted. I asked him what effect it might have on my sex life. And would you believe it? The guy actually blushed." Gynecologists and obstetricians often don't take women's feelings seriously, and they avoid sexual questions.

Until Masters and Johnson discovered that all orgasms women

experience were caused by clitoral stimulation, women bought the idea that there were two kinds of orgasms: the good kind and the bad kind. *Clitoral* orgasms were immature, so they were the wrong kind. *Vaginal* orgasms were the correct ones. This caused women psychological stress. Why couldn't they have the right kind of orgasm? Betty Friedan observed, "Instead of fulfilling the promise of infinite orgastic bliss, sex in the America of the feminine mystique is becoming a strangely joyless national compulsion, if not a contemporary mockery."*

Doctors were not the only ones to blame. Husbands like Blushing Betty's turned a deaf ear, too. The prevailing idea† was that a happy husband equals a happy wife. A wife is an extension of her husband, not a distinct person in her own right.

When a husband experienced a sexual problem—premature ejaculation or failure to maintain his erection—it was hard to hide from his wife. But a wife (even a "happily" married one) could easily cover up sexual difficulties. And she probably did. It was too delicate, too embarrassing, perhaps too castrating to complain about foreplay, orgasmic problems, or too little tenderness. Faking orgasm was their solution. "You were wonderful, the earth shook," they assured him. Faking orgasms became a national joke which stand-up comedians used in nightclubs from Vegas to Virginia. Women recognized its truth.

When sexual problems emerge, the entire relationship begins to suffer. Jane's 16-year marriage to a "perfect lover" ended when he became an alcoholic and sexual problems emerged. When Ada's husband raped her, that was the point at which she decided to reach out to Larry. Betty's husband forced her to perform in ways she found unpleasant, and soon sex became intolerable. This simply emphasized her lover's tenderness. A *New York Times* article‡ reported that most men were unaware their "happy" wives had any sex problems. According to Anthony Pietropinto and Jacqueline Simenauer, in *Beyond The Male Myth*, sex is not the male's most important pleasure. Four out of five men ranked work

* *The Feminine Mystique*, Ch. 11.
† The movie *Kramer versus Kramer* opened with this.
‡ July 21, 1978.

and success above sex. To women, this is not news. However, "Although wives might suffer their sexual dysfunctions in silence, sexual difficulties were apt to color the couple's relationship."

Sexual dysfunction can be a by-product of emotional or psychological problems, or a poor sex life can cause the emotional problem. It is not always easy to distinguish between cause and effect.

Sociologists Dr. David R. Mace and his wife Vera say, "The idea that it is the joy of sex that sustains a good marriage is putting the cart before the horse."° they claim that a good marriage sustains good sex. Redbook's survey concurs, ranking sex after love as factors in a happy marriage.

Nevertheless, younger women are less likely to suffer in silence and let the man direct the whole sexual show. Some are even educating and instructing their partners, as young wives become full participants in their sexual lives.

Shere Hite tells women that masturbation—far from being dirty or sinful—can help them achieve greater sexual pleasure. Does anyone still believe it will make you blind? Women learn that failure to reach orgasm may be a normal response to inadequate clitoral stimulation not provided by penetration in intercourse, that sex must be integrated into their lives and not be purely mechanistic.

Happily, the ballyhoo about vaginal and clitoral orgasms has been put to rest. Widely read books like *The Hite Report* by Shere Hite, *For Yourself: The Fulfillment of Female Sexuality* by Lonnie Garfield Barbach, and *The Redbook Report on Female Sexuality* by Carol Travis and Susan Sadd have added to women's perceptions of themselves, assuring them that they are not alone, not abnormal, and not crazy. Thousands of women have wrestled with the same sexual problems. "We're learning we are sexual in our own right, and that asking for sexual pleasure does not make us ball-breakers," confirms Betty-Jane Raphael in her *Ms.* article.†

Investigators have concluded that orgasm is only one aspect of sexual pleasure. They believe that orgasm, like sex itself, is never the whole picture. Perhaps some women who are happy in every

---

° *The New York Times,* April 20, 1977.
† "When He Says 'I Have A Headache' . . . ," September 1976.

other way—in their jobs, their lifestyles, and their marriages—
survive, even flourish, without orgasms. They still feel on top of the
world and they enjoy sexuality on other levels.

"Bullshit!" a saleswoman told me. "I couldn't live without sex and
that means orgasms to me. If they say it doesn't matter, it's because
they don't let it matter. They're fools. They don't know what
they're missing."

Ellen's affair with her "spiritual" lover was intense, romantic, but
totally without sex. Ellen would argue that the saleswoman was
wrong. Even without sex her affair was satisfying.

What turns a woman on to a particular lover? Jane found money
sexy; it represented power and achievement. Betty admitted to
simple desire; she wanted her lover, was sexually aroused. But then
she fell in love with him.

Both Jane and Betty found sex with their lovers a vast improve-
ment over sex with their husbands. Both claim that sex with a loving
partner is the ideal. A poor sex life within marriage may certainly
motivate a wife to seek pleasure elsewhere, but sex alone is probably not the only motivation.

Some married women find it necessary to believe they have
fallen in love with their lover. In fact, some of these marry their
lovers because marrying a lover takes the onus off the affair and
lessens guilt. If they marry their lover, the affair becomes
acceptable. The new marriage refutes the allegation that the affair
was based only on sex. It justifies breaking the trust and it takes the
sting out of the original betrayal. It implies a change of heart,
certainly, but a change based on love and codified by marital vows
made anew. And that is forgivable. As Jane and Betty testify, it's
hard to know what the dimensions of sex are—harder still to
separate sex from love. Good sex and bad sex are perceived in very
personal terms. Sexual acts that Betty called "terrible" and "dirty"
Jane called "fun" and "spontaneous."

The major sexual complaints—"not enough" and "too much"—
still defy measurement. Perhaps the therapist's joke says it best:

In the morning I see a patient who complains bitterly. "My husband
has lost interest in me, Doctor," she says. "How frequently do you

have sex?" I ask. "I'm ashamed to tell you. It's down to twice a week."

Later, I see another patient who complains bitterly, too. "My husband is an animal, Doctor. A sexual athlete. Nothing on his mind but sex, sex, sex." "How often do you have sex?" I ask. "I'm ashamed to tell you. Twice a week."

For women, and often for men too, sex and love are so closely tied they appear inseparable. The union of two bodies and the physical closeness after sex lead to an emotional closeness which is easily likened to love. For Jane and Betty what began as sex ripened into love.

And that is a very real danger in having an extramarital affair.

7

BOREDOM: CAROL

"GEORGE HAS ALWAYS been very good to me," Carol began. "A wonderful father, too. He's crazy about me. He'll do anything for me. My girlfriends would like to get the attention and devotion I've always had. It's ridiculous . . . but George still thinks I'm young and beautiful. My friends don't get that from their husbands—their husbands ignore them. So they envy my marriage."

Sounds wonderful, doesn't it? Yet despite this glowing picture, Carol—past fifty, mother of four—has a lover.

Why? Many wives in less fortunate positions would say Carol should have been grateful. What pushed this loved and appreciated woman to step out on her husband?

"I have nothing to say against him," she declared. "Nothing. He's a very good man. He just bores me."

Is boredom sufficient motivation to turn a wife against a husband of many years? Why is Carol repaying devotion this way? We may forgive the mistreated wife who has suffered indignities and pain over the years. Some may even applaud her and say "he had it coming!" If "A Good Man Is Hard to Find"—as Flannery O'Connor's short story informs us—why risk losing him? Is Carol a fool? Or an ingrate?

"My marriage was pleasant and comfortable. But *boring!* Boring, boring, boring. No adventure. No excitement. No fun. I took a lover to relieve the boredom. And also—let's be realistic—the circumstances were right. Everything fell into place.

"I was bored with my life. Bored with my husband. I craved excitement, a little pizzazz in my life. Then—just at the right moment—something happened. I wasn't out looking for it. So I don't feel guilty about this affair. I don't feel God's going to punish me. I've had a lover for seven years. And it's wonderful! It's exciting! It's fun!"

On the telephone, Carol's voice was urgent. I expected a soft, cultured voice—the woman taught English at a local college. Instead, I heard a quick gush of words. She left sentences unfinished and interrupted herself too.

"Meet me here. My home. Sure. Swell. Gotcha." No goodbye, she just hung up.

A reed-thin, fiftyish woman, in a fashionable pantsuit, opened the door. Her frosted blonde hair was styled in short springy curls. Despite the lines around her mouth and across her forehead, she looked like an adorable Shirley Temple on the Good Ship Lollipop.

She led me into a pleasantly cluttered living room, the walls covered with photographs, memorabilia, paintings, mirrors, and posters. A baby grand piano. A well-stocked bookcase. A sunny bay window full of hanging plants. Beckoning me to the couch, she pushed aside a bevy of throw pillows that seemed to draw together every color and texture in the room.

"Like them? I *made* them. Crewel. Bargello. Needlepoint. I do them all. In my spare time." A wide generous smile. "I've got lots of energy. I like to keep moving. But I don't bake," she apoligized, offering me a plate of "store-bought" cookies and freshly brewed coffee.

I turned the tape recorder on, and she plunged right in.

"I didn't suddenly wake up one morning and fall head over heels in love with Bruce. No. We were friends, the four of us, two married couples, for over twenty years. Bruce and his wife live on our block. It was the right timing and the right opportunity. *That's* when it happened. Boom!"

She made a gesture like a space ship taking off, then crossed her legs, continuing.

"I was 23 when I got married. My husband was 33—ten years older. George has always been my Daddy. He takes care of everything. I'm his little girl. All he ever wanted was a simple homemaker type like his mother. But I don't sit home. I go!

"I've been lucky, see? Lots of friends. Successful in my career. George feels insecure about it. But he's content in his way. He works hard—he has a stationery store—long hours. So he's happy to come home.

"When my four kids were small and I was stuck in all day, I'd have to fight for any club I joined. But finally, I wore him down. Now my time is my own. I do as I please.

"Look, many women begin an affair much earlier. I started late. I'm past fifty. And Bruce is my second lover. My first lover? Well, I'll tell you how it happened.

"My closest friend was my cousin. She had a very unhappy marriage, but she had children and didn't want to break up the marriage. I was her confidante. She could tell me about the troubles in her marriage, and she told me she had lovers. I admired her. She was a live wire, a little offbeat, less the nice acceptable suburban housewife. She told me she wouldn't allow herself to be locked into a miserable marriage. Her lovers kept her going. I would listen, entranced. And eventually she said of her current lover, 'Look, he has a friend'—a familiar story, right? I was frightened, but I said, 'Why not?' I was so bored.

"This man became my first lover. Was I dumb! Forty-three and I was Rebecca of Sunnybrook Farm. This man used me and left me after a year. I was sick over it. Depressed. Falling apart. Practically a mini-breakdown. I couldn't keep my mind on our work, on my home, on my children, on my husband. I couldn't function.

"The whole period I was recovering, George was absolutely wonderful. Of course, he had no idea why I couldn't sleep, but he'd walk the streets with me—one, two, three o'clock in the morning. I know he was secretly happy because I was sick. That meant I needed him. He could be my Big Daddy again.

"That's when Bruce and I changed our relationship. From friends to lovers.

Having It Both Ways

"Bruce is a salesman, my age exactly. His hours are erratic, and he's home a lot. I was home, too, writing my thesis. Despondent over the end of the affair. I remember it clearly. Friday. Bruce walked in calling, 'Coffee break.' But when he saw how depressed I was, he said, 'C'mon, I'll take you out to lunch.' It was a friendship thing—nothing more. We were neighbors. His wife knew we had lunch together sometimes, and so did George.

"Well, we started drinking. And I don't know what triggered it. I told him the whole ugly story—crying, sobbing, pouring it all out. How my lover had rejected me.

"He just listened. Quietly. Attentively. No judgments. 'I suspected an affair,' he said. 'I've been waiting for you to open up to me.' Then he took my hands in his. 'I've been yearning for you, hungry for you for years,' he told me.

"I wasn't eager to start another affair. But once you've had a lover, it's easier.

She laughs ruefully and continues unabashed.

"That Friday changed us from friends to lovers. Maybe I needed that flattery to recover. To be told I'm beautiful, desirable. Doesn't every woman need it? What I'm saying is: the timing was perfect. I was at my most vulnerable.

"That was seven years ago. I see Bruce every day. We'll never stop seeing each other. Being friends increases our opportunities to be together. At 50, you find a friend for a lover. I did. Right on my own block.

"I didn't decide to snag a man, to pick up a guy at a bar. It was timing and circumstances. They all came together: a boring marriage, a need for excitement, and my feeling so depressed.

"George sees me only in a certain light. He doesn't have the excitement I crave. Intellectually. Culturally. Sexually.

"Sex with George was never fantastic. But I was too innocent to know better. I thought sex was something wives did for their husbands. I thought a wife owes it to her husband for all the things he gives her. Maybe it was a trade-off for security. We never talked about sex, we just did it. If he did something that didn't please me, I'd never say a word. Why bother? I didn't find him attractive.

After 28 years, what surprises are left? The same body, in the same bed, night after night. Is that romantic? B-o-o-r–ring!

"The question is, why did I marry George? I've thought about it a lot. He was certainly the opposite of my father. My father was a very attractive man. Very bright. He had a lot of women. When my mother died—it was the same week I met George—my father replaced her right away. I felt he was disloyal to my mother. I needed time to grieve with my father. I resented another woman, but he brought her in right away. I had to get married. To get out of that house.

"George was certainly good to me, I can't deny it. It was important for me to know that he'd always be there to take care of me. I guess I needed a Daddy. And at first I was busy raising the kids. And that was enough for me. I had my hobbies, my club, I took courses. I had many friends.

"But after twenty years of marriage you begin to want more— more adventure. See, an affair is full of excitement. And fun! There's the excitement leading up to meeting your lover. All the planning. Getting dressed for him. The secrecy. The excitement keeps me way up there. All keyed up. High.

"Why don't I leave George? I did. Last year, past fifty. I left. I knew if I was ever going to make the move, it would have to be now. I went to a divorce lawyer and you know what she told me? 'If you want a divorce, you have to move out.' I *love* my house. I couldn't move. Divorce meant going to some lonely little apartment.

"George wouldn't move either. He was smart not to move. He didn't even ask me if there was someone else. Bruce was against the divorce, too. Maybe he figured I'd find another man—an available, unmarried man. I thought it over carefully. There was no one out there waiting for me. I'd be going away all by myself.

"So I thought: Well, I can have all this . . . the house, safety, companionship. And I can go on seeing Bruce. Maybe my marriage wasn't exciting. But it was pleasant. It was secure. Why make waves?

"When George asks, 'Want a cup of tea, hon?' I remind myself, 'Isn't this better than being alone?' I see lots of single women out there—divorced, widowed—it's no picnic. Alone is lousy.

"I could have made the move years ago. But it's too late now. I couldn't start over. Divorce is not the solution.

"Bruce and I have a marvelous time together. We laugh constantly. We're like 16-year-old kids. We have so much in common. We meet for lunch or after school almost every day. He waits for me in the school parking lot. Sometimes I think *ours* is the marriage.

"And sometimes, for excitement, I break up with Bruce."

She laughs heartily. She is a woman who can laugh at herself.

"It's childish, I guess. He sends flowers to the school and I pretend it's from George. It's exciting. Romantic. An affair can have all the good parts—none of the bad parts—of marriage. That's the difference. Your lover doesn't pay the bills. No obligations. No hassles. I don't think we'll ever stop seeing each other.

"Bruce has given me a dimension I could never have with George. I feel free. I do things—sexual things—I'd never do with my husband. I'm so turned on by Bruce. I wait all day to be with him. We get dressed up for each other. Buy funny little gifts—something silly, for a laugh. The sex is so good. But it's not only sex that turns me on. It's the feeling I have about him. I love him—even if I do pick a fight for a little excitement. He loves me. It gets better and stronger every year. We take holidays together, do everything together. Bruce has enhanced my whole life.

"I know married women who live far away from their lovers. They have to sneak around, make elaborate plans to be together. Their lover is not part of their everyday life.

"You're probably thinking that I come on strong, right? I know I do. But underneath I'm a passive person. That's why I admired my cousin. She found compensations for a bad marriage. But I stay with George. Let's face it: The status and economics of being married have their advantages. I stay married because it's comfortable.

"Of course, there is some risk. But that's part of the excitement. The risk is a turn-on to me. Having a lover happens to be incredible fun. Even the risk is fun.

"It's seven years and the excitement is still there. Someone might catch us in a motel—you never know. We go to motels miles away.

They're cheater places, so whoever's there is cheating, too. It's easy for me because I'm always on the run. College teaching is no nine-to-five job. There are meetings and conferences, appointments, and office hours. I make my own schedule. And there are my friends. I can always call one up and say, 'Look, say I'm with you, okay?' They cover for me.

"If my children found out, I wouldn't deny it. They're no babies anymore, and they understand the realities of life. They love their father, but I think they would be sympathetic.

"Because the four of us are best friends, there's little risk in neighborhood gossip. If Bruce walks over or parks his car in front of my house, so what? He's a friend. We never sleep together in my house. Oh, no. Never. As far as the world is concerned, we're friends. Nothing wrong in that.

"When I spend a night with him or go away for a weekend, that's riskier. It requires more care, more planning. I hate to tell you the low tactics I've resorted to."

She's embarrassed, and gets up to pick a few leaves off a Swedish ivy.

"Okay, okay, I'll tell you. I've used Bruce's wife. She goes to California every July to see her family. I tell her, 'Look, say I'm going with you.' I make up a teacher's convention, an English seminar. She probably knows I'm having an affair, but she doesn't pry. Using her is my perfect alibi. I feel uncomfortable, but then I go to meet Bruce anyhow.

"Sometimes when I speak to my girlfriends who are really down, so bored—I think every woman should have at least one affair. It's important for a woman of a certain age to have a lover. I'm getting older. I'm losing my looks. And it takes a lot to have an affair. The lying can be tricky. You can forget what you've said. If you make a slip, you have to think fast to cover up. It takes a bit of conniving. You have to be well physically. You need a lot of pep and go. But it's worth it! Look what you're getting. Excitement. Pleasure. Sex. An intimate, beautiful relationship. Love. Fun. Adventure.

"I know plenty of women who would love an affair. Don't you? But they're afraid. Or they don't know how to go about it. One woman—she teaches two other sections of Freshman Comp—told me, 'Gee, I wish I had a guy. I wish I had a lover.' She's only 29! Married only eight years. Another—a student in my nine o'clock class—was absent for the midsemester exam. She looked terrible when she came back. 'Baby sick?' I asked her. 'No, *I'm* sick. I'm thinking about a love affair.' She's a ripe old 32. Young women. They're scared to try it. But they probably will.

"When I hear my friends bitching, I think, 'I know what they need.' They need a little excitement. A little romance. A lover! What's wrong? If your husband doesn't know, it doesn't hurt.

"I like my life now. I've learned to maintain two lives and to balance them. George is past sixty. I can't say 'satisfy me sexually, I need more sex.' For sex and romance I have Bruce.

"I've had it both ways for seven years. Doesn't that prove something?"

❂   ❂   ❂

To hear Carol tell it, boredom and marriage are unavoidable—they go hand in hand. And boredom *can* drive a woman to take a lover. This may seem unacceptable to some.

But change Carol's name to Charles and the situation is suddenly explicable. Boredom has always provided husbands with the perfect excuse for cheating. A wife may be an excellent housekeeper, a fine mother, his hostess, bookkeeper, chauffeur, gardener, cook, and so forth. But if she's also boring, a man may be given license to look for excitement in another woman's arms. He will be excused. Boredom, for a man, is an acceptable motivation.

Carol's statement, "What's wrong? If your husband doesn't know, it doesn't hurt," is what men have been saying all along.

As Dr. Joyce Brothers writes, "Marriage is not just spiritual communion and passionate embraces; marriage is also three-meals-a-day and remembering to carry out the trash."* Is Carol merely a cynic? Is she bitter? Is there any validity to her claims?

A 32-year-old dental assistant, married nine years, talked with me and echoed Dr. Brothers:

"I got married because I was in love. But you find out soon enough that being in love—that terrific romantic feeling of walking on clouds—well, it's just incompatible with the day-to-day business

---

*"When Your Husband's Affection Cools," *Good Housekeeping*, May 1972.

of marriage. The passion goes down the drain with the dishwater. And if you wind up with a cozy feeling for each other after a few years—well, count yourself lucky."

Although she didn't want to be interviewed on tape, she told me:

"I'm not dissatisfied with my marriage, and I'm sexually well adjusted. But I enjoy the excitement of feeling in love again. Marriage gets boring, and the excitement of a new man keeps me going. I know it can't last forever—affairs come to an end. And I want to keep my husband. But when boredom sets in, an extramarital affair soothes me over the bumps.

"But I don't want to leave my husband. I'd be crazy to trade him in. He's a nice man. We've got two little kids. It surprises me that I don't feel guilty. Everyone wants a little extra. That's how I get mine."

We all know couples who started out in white heat: a whirlwind romance—all passion and fire. The bridegroom couldn't keep his hands off his bride. He was forever stroking her, nuzzling her, touching her. They leaned toward each other like plants bending toward the sun. They did everything together. It was Phil-'n-Jane—one word—like ham 'n eggs. You didn't think of them as separate persons. If you flip through the pages of their old photo album, you can see how she clings to him, how he wraps himself around her. God, they were in love!

Follow up the loving couple ten, fifteen years later—if they're still together. They're raising children, moving up in their careers. They've gone through a lot together. They're a family now. Notice how the relationship has cooled. What did it? Many would agree with Carol: Marriage. The curse of the three M's: marriage means monotony.

They may still like each other, even be devoted companions. But what happened to all that white heat? Sunday mornings they used to spend in bed, making love. Now he'd rather play tennis; she'd rather plant tomatoes. Sex is so available, so convenient, so dull. Routine has eroded romance.

Long-married couples, even hand-holding ones, sometimes acquire new labels for each other to redefine the partnership. Instead of "angel," "baby," and "sweetheart," they call each other

"Mother" and "Dad." They may be genuinely fond of each other, but romance and excitement are no longer central forces in their relationship. Where once the most insistent ingredients were sexual tension and excitement, the day-to-day business of marriage has rewritten the recipe. Now the largest ingredients—if they are lucky—are friendship and good will, which cement their bonds. Romance may appear as an afterthought, an occasional bouquet of flowers, an anniversary dinner alone, a special birthday present. All are conscious attempts to keep romance alive.

For many couples, the arrangement is satisfactory, and they are grateful for those intermittent sparks of romance. They are realists. They recognize that the familiar inevitably loses its appeal. They grumble, but they accept it and busy themselves with other interests. They find excitement in a new skill, a hobby, a sport. They may return to college, study a musical instrument, take up racquetball.

And they look around for reassurance. Are they alone? No, it happens to everyone. On television, husbands read newspapers with their breakfast coffee. Spouses who ask, "How was your day, dear?" don't listen to the answer. Disinterest and boredom seem to be rampant in American homes.

Some couples measure their friends' happiness against their own. Women at home and at work compare notes. Men in gym locker rooms kid each other about "how many times." Soon enough they find out it is the same for most married couples. Passion soars with separation and novelty—the literature is full of examples: Romeo and Juliet; Tristan and Isolde. But where are the flaming romances between couples living together 10, 20, or 30 years?

In his book *Coming Together, Coming Apart*, Dr. Jay Kuten, assistant professor of psychiatry at Boston University School of Medicine, says that sexual interest among married couples wanes with togetherness, and this can become a burden. He finds it a paradox that lovers long for togetherness; then, having achieved it, find passion flees. Boredom sets in.

College students living in close proximity in co-ed dorms have expressed similar feelings. "How can I feel romantic about the dude I pass in the hall every morning on his way to the john?" a sophomore at Ithaca College told me. Young men and women brought up in Israeli kibbutzim echo the same feelings. "Date Etan? Don't be ridiculous. He seems more like a brother to me."

A couple may have a close friendship, even a deep commitment to each other. But for those who cannot accept the diminishing of romance, dissatisfactions loom like storm clouds over the marriage. Like Carol, they may need more.

A love affair may be the answer.

"Look, it's hard to feel excited about a husband when you've been dropping his dirty underwear into the washing machine for twelve years," a part-time researcher told me. "Somehow the glamour and excitement drown under the soapsuds." Like the dental assistant, she found extra excitement in affairs.

Helen Singer Kaplan, M.D., Ph.D., is Director of the Human Sexuality Program at Payne Whitney Clinic in New York. In a column in *Savvy* magazine,* she talks about boredom. Does she agree that the same body can't possible stay exciting over the years? Even in a *happy* marriage? "Oh, that's definitely not true," she writes. "The common myth that monogamy doesn't satisfy one's sexual needs is bull . . . there's no such thing as sexual boredom—boredom is a sign of hidden anger or mistrust."

A travel agent who specializes in booking expensive, luxurious trips abroad told me the rich and the bored pay her office rent, her overhead, and buy her a new car.

"I have a number of clients—women of means—who regularly go to Europe alone or with other women. In a few weeks of travel, they renew themselves and they're content to come home to a boring husband. I've met a few of those husbands. They may be satisfactory socially—they're nice looking, tanned, well dressed. But you can tell the excitement is gone and their wives are bored. A little hanky-panky sailing on the QE2 seems to lift the wives' spirits and keeps them going. If they can afford it—who am I to discourage them?"

> When an American heiress wants to buy a man, she at once crosses the Atlantic.
>
> Mary McCarthy, "On the Contrary," 1961

*"The Varied Purposes of the Extramarital Affair," May 1980.

Having It Both Ways

I asked the travel agent if her clients ever discuss their trips when they come back. "Most don't, they're discreet. But a few—they've become friends over the years—they're pretty open. A stockbroker's wife told me that finding a new romance works better than penicillin. She said, 'A new man is a sure-fire aphrodisiac.' Another woman—her husband is retired and goes fishing, which she hates—came back from Spain looking radiant, and told me, 'A new man in my life. Guaranteed to kill the blues.' One woman—enormously wealthy, her husband owns a string of hotels—said, 'Who cares what's on the menu for the Captain's Dinner? What I want to know is what unattached men are on the passenger list!'"

The lure of the new is always exciting. Every woman understands how a new dress can lift her spirits. A new car, a new job, a new home—most new things are powerful morale builders. They gain your attention; they spark up your hopes; they invite your best efforts. A new man—particularly if the wife feels locked into a boring or unsatisfactory marriage—can do the same. The element of newness can work as a powerful stimulant.

Carol says: "It's seven years and the excitement is still there."

Ada says her affair was an energizer: "I had so much energy, it was unbelievable."

"Glorious," "wonderful," and "idyllic," are the words wives use to describe a new love affair.

There is nothing more evocative for a woman than to be desired. If a man says, as Bruce said to Carol, "I've hungered for you for years," she may find herself almost automatically reassessing her feelings for him. For twenty years Bruce had been Carol's friend. It was not until he expressed his hunger for her that she allowed herself to think of him sexually. His arousal created her arousal, or allowed it to emerge. She now felt free to respond in kind. Her friend became her lover.

And so the relationship changes. The affair begins.

Until recently, men have traditionally been the ones to take the cure. When an attack of male menopause hit, when an over 40 husband could no longer perform as often or as well with his wife of many seasons, his response to this distress was to seek "outside" relief. Someone else would surely turn him on. Someone younger and slimmer. A flatter stomach, tighter thighs, or larger breasts would do the trick. But if these were unobtainable, *someone new* might work just as well. Freud called it *Türschlusspanik* (the closing-door panic—)the need to have a final fling, before it's too late.

Women are not immune. We heard it in Carol's story when she said, "Look, I'm getting older. I'm losing my looks."

A woman in Austin, Texas, told me, "Sure, the excitement of a new partner feels good. But you have to forget his flaws. While everything is so bright and shiny, you look the other way. He's new. He wants to please you. You want to please him. So you forgive those less than perfect moments."

In Herbert Gold's novel *He/She*, the nameless wife is seeking a life of "unboredom." Her husband is trying to make their marriage a "festival." Like so many contemporary women of the 80s, it is the wife who takes the initiative. She makes her own plans. Something is nagging her. She wants to cure the " . . . sense of error in her life." What is it? She's bored with her husband. Once in a while she allows him to make love to her. But he no longer excites her.

Novels, movies, and plays all make generous use of this plot. Adultery is America's Number One Hidden Fantasy.

The message is clear. Marriage is okay. A necessary institution that eventually becomes boring. But an affair is dynamite. Smart people—in books and plays and movies—have it both ways. As Carol said: "My husband for a Daddy. My lover for excitement ." The 100 percent solution.

Those writing on extramarital affairs have focused their attention particularly on the male. Dr. Edmond C. Hallberg's book calls it *The Gray Itch*. Nancy Mayer's book calls it *The Male Mid-Life Crisis*. The distress men feel around 40 or 50 is now part of popular literature. Temptation itself is everywhere. At 40 or 50 comes the awareness that life is too brief.

One out of two men will merely fantasize about adultery, honor their marriage vows, and be faithful. The other half of that statistic—*Every Other Man* according to psychiatrist Dr. Mary Ann Bartusis' book—will cheat.

"Well, I've got news for you," a 36 year old woman law student told me. "Extramarital balling isn't exclusively a male reaction. It relieves my tension. It gets me out of my marital rut. I couldn't get through law school without it."

Women's magazines devote considerable attention to the quest for romance. Many of their issues feature at least one lead article on the subject: "How to Renew Your Husband's Sexual Appetites"; "What An Affair Can Do to Your Marriage"; "The Sensible Way to Handle Infidelity." While the flip titles are calculated to ensnare readers, these articles are designed to be cheerful and uplifting; they offer heartfelt advice, perhaps concluding with "Your Ten Point Plan to Spice Up a Ho-Hum Marriage." Take a trip together, lose weight, buy sexy lingerie.

Rarely is the solution: have an affair. What if the operation is a success, but the patient dies?

Dr. Shirley Zussman, vice president of the American Association of Sex Educators, Counsellors and Therapists, claims that she has never come across an "open marriage" that worked. She considers it an intellectual football people enjoy tossing around. As a lifestyle, she says, open marriage is not viable.

William Lederer, author of *The Mirages of Marriage*, states that "a happy, workable, productive marriage does not require love," that it is impossible to live in a permanent state of romance. If we experience love 10 percent of the time and treat each other with courtesy, says Lederer, chances are the marriage will endure.

But is endurance the goal? Most of us are impassioned romantics at heart. We hope we will be in love with our husbands forever, but that condition rarely prevails.

Jennie Jerome Churchill (1851–1921), who fluttered many a heart on both sides of the Atlantic, pointed this out in "His Borrowed Plumes."

Alma: I rather suspect her of being in love with him.
The reply by Martin is a shocking, "Her own husband?"

8

CRISES: GINA

WHEN SEXUAL DIFFICULTIES, loss of a job, death of a parent, a blow to self esteem, depression, job relocation, children's problems, or illnesses become crises, they can exact a heavy toll on a marriage.

Most of us get married to stay married. Newlyweds believe they are inured against crisis and tragedy. They don't anticipate unemployment, illness, or other problems that will seriously affect their marriage. Crises happen to *other* people in the newspapers and on the six o'clock news. Whether a relationship survives crises and is strengthened by them, or is overturned by the first wave of trouble, depends largely on who the partners are, how they deal with adversity, and other resources in their emotional arsenal.

Solving problems that were unimaginable to couples as newlyweds can help cement the relationship. However, when massive disappointments strike—chronic illness, shattering discoveries of betrayals, job and sexual stresses, problems over children and aging parents, alcoholism, unemployment, infidelity, and death—serious strains are placed on the marriage. Then, even the best marriages may struggle to survive, or may continue as a legal entity, where, for all practical purposes, the couple lead separate lives. Even a "moderately unhappy" couple may opt to continue a less than perfect marriage. But they seek compensation elsewhere. *One out of three wives takes a lover.* For many women, an overwhelming crisis heralds their first love affair.

What issues put the most strain on couples, what crises touch most families and motivate wives to take lovers?

Traditionally, newlyweds make a transition in their twenties from living as their parents' children to becoming a husband or wife. Each carries in his and her head their parents' values and idiosyncrasies. If couples have not lived together before, the wedding day may mark the beginning of an evolving discovery of the spouse's imperfections. "Hang up your clothes," "Put the toilet seat down," and "Get off the phone" are only minor skirmishes. If they *have* lived together, problems may still emerge. The wedding commitment is a final one, and a wife can no longer harbor the image of a perfect future lover who will satisfy her in every way. Her spouse must now fulfill that image. The flaws she overlooked in a live-in lover now require negotiation and compromise.

Far more difficult, according to Maggie Scarf, author of the book *Unfinished Business,* are the serious psychological tasks of making and breaking emotional bonds. The new wife must reconcile her need for autonomy with the pull to form close attachments to her husband and children. To forge and adjust these bonds while still remaining close to her parents requires flexibility. Often the need to be independent conflicts with the need to be close. If a young wife cannot transfer primary loyalty from her parents to her husband, trouble is bound to brew. Women must do the work of attaching and separating at key moments in their lives, Scarf says, or else they remain "stuck" and they risk depression. In the twenties, when to have children can become a battleground. What kind of birth control to use can become a dispute that affects sexual intimacy.

"I took the pill for two years," a 26-year-old chemist said, "and John was content because it was my responsibility. But when I read about the side effects, I got scared and I switched to a diaphragm. It was so damn messy, once it shot right across the room. So I asked John to use the good, old-fashioned rubber. And boy, did he fume. He refused. So I refused. It was one solid week of stand-offs. Until hot lust got in the way."

Crises: Gina

A 29-year-old former photographer's model talked about her quarrel with her husband over money. "Wayne isn't a bit verbal on other issues, but when it came to money he has no trouble shooting off his big mouth. Before the kids came, I worked and we pooled our money. But now I have to go to him for every cent. It's a constant battle. He uses money to punish me and reward me, and I resent it. I want my own money."

The thirties and forties is the time when most marriages break up. When a wife feels cheated—sexually, financially, or emotionally—and she feels powerless in her marriage, she is more likely to find solace in an extramarital affair.

Feeling trapped is not uncommon among wives in their thirties and forties. These are stressful years. Husbands are busy climbing to the top. Working wives are often doing two full-time jobs, juggling the demands of the home against a job. Emotionally and financially, the pressures of child rearing are greatest during these years. There are cars to be paid off, mortgages and insurance bills due, and often couples feel they can never get ahead, even if the wife goes back to work.

Wives who stay home experience different problems. If the family depends on the husband's salary, the wife's total reliance on her husband may cause loss of esteem and independence. A salaried worker always pulls more points. Housework is caretaker's work, and caretakers are rarely valued. A husband may compliment his wife publicly on her prudent food shopping and their lovely home, but the highest priority is still accorded the breadwinner.

This produces—with rare exception—definite inequities. The man who pays the piper calls the tune. If the husband is the sole wage earner, he generally has the most to say about how the money will be spent. The undercurrent is: It's *my* money. I earned it. I say how we spend it. Even a generous allowance carries less weight psychologically than earned money. This is why husbands whose wives earn more than they often suffer loss of self-esteem, even sexual impotence. Dependence on one paycheck—the husband's—makes him a necessity. If he loses his job, where will the money come from? What will happen to his family?

In a one-paycheck family, loss of employment constitutes a serious crisis in a marriage. According to *The Wall Street Journal,*° "Recessions may be hazardous to your health."

"A 22-year-old Detroit auto worker was laid off by General Motors last year. His wife became pregnant and the couple worried that the baby would be born deformed because their diet had deteriorated. The man was hospitalized with a nervous breakdown, but had to leave the hospital when his health insurance ran out in April. Distraught, he drove home and hanged himself."†

An upper-middle-class dentist's wife reveals her terror when her successful husband decided to give up dentistry.

"I figured the man was going through some kind of mid-life crisis. He said dentistry wasn't for him anymore, and he wanted to change careers. He yearned to become a photographer and to camp out under the stars and capture nature. He wanted to escape the root canals and the nitrous oxide. Fine. Great. For him! But what happens to us? Two kids in college and a wife who hasn't worked for twenty-five years? I was terrified. I told him to see a shrink."

This dentist *chose* to give up his profession. However, when the sole breadwinner is fired, the repercussions can be felt beyond the wallet. Loss of a job can cause loss of self-esteem, withdrawal, and depression, with reverberations which can be felt in the bedroom.

"When my husband was fired from his teaching job several months ago, he took it very hard. Although it was a case of cutting back due to lowered enrollments, he took it as a personal rejection. Until that day, we had no problems in bed. He initiated sex twice a week or more. The day he was fired, everything changed. I think he could go without sex forever. He has no interest in it and twice, when I initiated sex, he was impotent. I tried to kid him out of it. I said you may have lost your job, but does that mean I lost my sex partner? He gave me a look that could kill."

When Betty's husband was laid off from the airlines, it had a serious impact upon their lives. Initially, its consequences were emotional, but soon it was felt in their sexual encounters, too.

° August 25, 1980.
† Ibid.

When Jane's husband had a heart attack and became an alcoholic and stopped working, she could not weather the crisis.

Job relocation affects about 500,000 employees every year, and can cause a serious upheaval for the wife. Even if relocation means a promotion and a substantial pay raise, it can place a heavy burden upon the family. Children are often frightened about finding new friends and enrolling in a new school. Wives have to find new jobs, leave parents and dear friends. No matter how attractive the company makes it—interest free loans, $1,000 gifts for down payments—the benefit package usually doesn't make up for the emotional toll. Breaking long-established ties and having to adjust to a whole new environment, new friends, and a new life is frightening. If the wife balks about pulling up stakes, a "commuter marriage" may be the result, in which the couple rendezvous only when career priorities permit.

A 23-year-old statistician reported that his wife of less than a year was initially very upset about moving out of New York. So was he. He felt he'd miss "everything about New York from the New York Jets football games to the beaches." But for these newlyweds, without children and long-standing ties, there were compensations which could make the adjustment easier. The young man saw it as "a chance to become a homeowner."* So the relocation might be a hurdle, but not an insurmountable one.

For older couples in their thirties and forties, uprooting from their community can cause a more severe crisis. If it is the *wife's* job that requires relocation, the schism can be even worse. It is the rare husband who is willing to relocate for his wife's promotion.

Job pressures are most severe during the thirties and forties, while careers are being forged. For the woman married to a chief executive, the burdens are enormous. Her husband is probably putting in a 60-hour week, traveling extensively, and under unrelieved pressure to produce. She's left alone to cope with small children and large problems. In the early days of the marriage, she might be willing to make the necessary sacrifices, because the pay-off seems so attractive when she's young and starting out. A

* *The Wall Street Journal*, August 15, 1980.

bigger house, a maid, charge accounts, cars, and clothes are powerful incentives. Until the resentments accumulate. The crisis may not appear for many years, but it almost always surfaces.

Weekends are set aside to cram in all of the living the family failed to do throughout the week. The social activities, the emotional support, the lovemaking other couples enjoy unfettered by time pressures are jammed into those two days. And sometimes, even the weekend is cut out when the chief executive is called on to give up Saturday or Sunday for a business meeting or a seminar in a distant city. As a result, the couple's relationship deteriorates, and so does the husband's relationship with his children.

"I had a son and two daughters I didn't even know," a Fortune 500 executive reports. "And I spent 60 percent of my time away from my wife. It began to show. We had nothing to talk about after the first hour of catching up. How do you recapture what happened to you last week? The telephone helps, but the moment is stale, gone, over. She couldn't understand my work pressures and I couldn't understand her complaints."

A wife recalls the stress her husband's position put on her ego. "I was not a person. I was just the chief's wife. The fact that I was a damn good sculptor faded into the background. No one talked to me or got to know me. I was introduced as his missus. No one knew my first name or cared."

Another woman describes marriage to an executive as "absentee marriage." "He's never around. Business comes first; his personal needs like golf come next; and at the bottom of the totem pole comes me. Well, how do you think that makes me feel?"

A corporate chief admits: "I missed my son's graduation and my daughter's school play. Just couldn't make it. I've lost touch with my family, but there's no way out. Once you live high on the hog, it's hard to go back."

In a survey based on interviews with 306 chief executives of the country's 1,300 largest corporations, respondents candidly revealed that their family life suffered. And the pressures become greater the closer they get to the top. The executive's wife not only suffers loneliness and personal resentment, she also feels the additional stress of trying to be two people—a mother and a father.

"He was never around when I needed him," a 42-year-old sales representative for a medical supply house explained. "So I found a substitute to give my boys a male role model. It started out when Warren came over to help the kids build model airplanes. But then after I put them to bed, we looked at each other and said, Why not? Warren gives us more than my husband does. Emotionally, socially, and sexually, I get a lot out of the affair. My husband can go on paying the bills. That's all he's good for."

Resentment over an absentee husband, who robs her of years of companionship and closeness, is often the start of an impending crisis. When a wife is lonely, resentful, and fatigued, a love affair makes it all seem bearable.

❀   ❀   ❀

Gina was such a woman. Married for years to an executive vice president of an important, listed public company, she experienced many of the problems common to women married to the man at the top. She felt lonely, trapped, isolated, without support. She also carried the burden of her own full-time job, a household, and two children for whom she was largely responsible.

Gina lived in a luxury high-rise at a fashionable East Side address overlooking Central Park in New York. She had canceled our appointment twice, but this time she answered and told the doorman to send me right up.

"I'm so sorry." She stood at the door holding her robe closed. "I was in the shower. Come in."

While she dressed, I looked about. The foyer, living room, and dining room flowed one into the other, offering a breathtaking view of the park. There was an extensive art collection—sculpture pieces in bronze, metal, and carved wood placed dramatically on marble pedestals; paintings, vases, tapestries and wall hangings; molas and mirrors—a veritable museum. Persian rugs on the parquet floors and hand-designed wallpapers in the foyer. I recognized a Matisse drawing over the velvet sofa, a Picasso, and a Chagall.

"Limited editions," she explained. "The Picasso is number 122 of 200. But the large sculptures are all originals, collected from Africa and Europe. Wherever we travel, we pick up something."

She was a petite woman, braless and barefoot, with huge dark eyes like black olives, and a sallow complexion. Mid-forties,

139

unsmiling, businesslike, but strikingly beautiful. She pushed back her dark, short cropped hair, tucked one foot under her, and sat down on the sofa.

"My mother lives with me now, my father died six years ago. She went out for her newspaper and a walk, so," she glanced at her watch, "we have about an hour and a half. Okay?"

"I met Edward when I was 37, and we've been lovers for ten years. But it's not the usual love affair. We only see each other four or five times a year because he lives in San Francisco. We meet here in the city or in almost any city in the world. We've rendezvoused in Washington, Paris, Rome, Tel Aviv. . . .

"Edward's a brilliant scientist. He invented an important new drug. He's also a champion skier. We meet in Switzerland for the slopes. He also paints, and he's a musician. I was 37. He was 45, married with four children. Every time we get together it's new and exciting. Last year I saw him in Cambridge, England, and we often meet in Washington because he's there a few times a year trying to get F.D.A. approval on various drugs. We've also developed a family friendship. When his children come to New York, they stay with me. It's not your typical love affair. Though I met Edward through very ordinary circumstances.

"He was in New York visiting his brother and sister-in-law, who were friends of mine. They knew my husband was away again on another business trip and that I was alone. So they invited me to join them for dinner and the theater. And they brought Edward along.

"He saw me home and came up for a few drinks. And that very night, he wanted me to sleep with him. I wasn't shocked. But I turned him down cold, though we talked until four A.M. Actually, I found him very appealing and extremely attractive, and I was flattered that he spent most of the evening trying to persuade me to go to bed with him. He had traveled extensively, and we had so much to talk about. Places we'd been, hotels, restaurants, concerts, theater. He also had a keen interest in art and appreciated my collection.

"He was writing and giving papers all over the world. And I was in publishing, so we had all that to talk about, too. I was an editor for a woman's magazine. I've worked there full time since college.

This was February, a bleak cold winter, and I was stuck in New York with two kids—they were eight and ten—while my husband was in sunny Spain for six weeks. I was resentful. Both kids were sick that winter and I couldn't take it anymore. It turned into a full-blown fight that we couldn't resolve.

"Anyhow, I had six months to think about Edward. He wrote to me and told me he was giving a paper in Tel Aviv in July. Would I join him there? He wrote to me again from Israel and I wrote back and we set it up. My husband had a business trip to the same country coming up too, so I went to Israel early and stayed on a kibbutz with the kids waiting for my husband to meet me there.

"I told Edward where I'd be and he just showed up, came to the kibbutz, and that's when the relationship started—during those two weeks when my husband wasn't there. Since then . . . it's funny . . . all four of us have become friends. His wife and my husband . . . the four of us.

"This is one of the best things that ever happened to me. It adds an extra dimension to my life and we know neither of us would leave our spouses. My husband is an executive with the international division of a vitamin company. He has to do a lot of traveling, I mean a lot. See all those masks and vases? The wood carving, the tapestries—all from China, Japan, India, South America, Europe. He sets up companies in different parts of the world. He travels three to four months a year, about four to six weeks each trip. Right from the beginning I was left home with two little kids. I was also working full time, and all the responsibilities for the kids were on my head. I had a housekeeper, but who signs them up for dance classes and takes them to the orthodontist? Me. Who deals with a broken ankle iceskating and lost eyeglasses? Me."

She sighs—a long, tired sigh, and for the moment she seems frail and waiflike.

"My husband is interesting in his way. But the level of excitement in any marriage dulls after a few years. And the traveling and pressures of his position didn't help. Marriage to a top executive is no bed of roses. We've had some marital problems over it. I felt resentful. He was having a more exciting life than I was. I was

141

saddled with all the responsibilities. He was married to his damn company. His salary is in six figures with a generous expense account and extras galore, but the company extracts their full value from him, believe me. We had periods of total sexual abstinence even after he'd come back from a long trip. I don't know if I was getting back at him or he was getting back at me. Every time he went on another trip, it was a crisis because I was left home alone.

"The years that you're raising small children are very pressured years. My daughter started all her acting out while her father was traveling. And my son was not doing well in school. They were pressure years, tough hard years. I was trying to run a household. My parents were aging and required attention. Then a tragedy changed the course of my brother's life. His wife was killed in a freak boating accident, so I helped him take care of his family, too. There were too many areas of stress, too many crises, and they took a toll on the general excitement in our marriage. It became . . . almost a business relationship. How are we dealing with this? With that? Did your mother get to the doctor? Did the prescription get filled? Did you sister sell the condo? Did the lawyer do this or that? Too many outside problems. One crisis after another. No time for us. No time to relate. All the daily pressures with kids piled up, and as soon as we got past one hurdle, there was another one. If he was on a trip, I had to attend to it alone. I was so tired, always tired.

"I was very young when I got married and my husband was like a lot of men during the 1950s. His generation idealized the woman. She's a good little girl so she can't get too involved sexually. They put the wife and the mother on a pedestal, so they didn't try anything experimental in bed. Even to this day, that hasn't changed. Routine sex. It's always in the bedroom. It's always on the bed. It's always late at night with the lights off. With a lover . . . Edward taught me . . . oral sex."

Having touched on the subject of sex, she veers off in another direction.

"Even if I don't see Edward, he calls me every three or four weeks. Or he writes to me at the office. I pick up my mail every day. It's funny. . . . When I initially met Edward, I was at a critical point in my life. I was saying, 'Who knows what my husband is doing on all those trips?' Though I never had evidence of anything. But you wonder. And I began to think, 'Why shouldn't I have a little icing on the cake? My husband is gone and he's having a very fulfilling life with his traveling.' He would come back and regale me with wonderful stories about the things he bought and the interesting people he met. And I was home trapped. Maybe there was hostility, too. I knew women who said it was fun to have a lover. So I thought . . . Everybody's doing it. Why not me?

"Even if the sex ended, I'd still want to be Edward's friend. We laugh a lot, we talk a lot. A man like Edward isn't easy to come across. This is a fluke, and I think it's very good for my ego. A lover keeps you on your toes. He keeps you looking more attractive. I know a lot of friends who are frustrated, unhappy, a little bored with their husbands, and I think a lover is good advice. It keeps life more exciting. When you hit 40, you worry about aging.

"My husband would be crushed if he found out. He wouldn't take it lightly. But he won't. If a woman has a lover close by, it's hard to hide. But it works beautifully for us because we live so far apart. When Edward and I became lovers, I said, 'Why did I have to meet somebody from San Francisco?' And he said, 'No, no, it's the best thing. In New York, we'd have to sneak around.' He was right.

"No, I don't feel guilty, and it's been over ten years. I don't believe I'm hurting anybody, and I think it's keeping me happier. In a way, it's making me a better wife and mother. I don't consider myself a typical middle-class housewife. I've worked all my life. I've traveled. I live a sophisticated life. And I know a lot of women who have lovers.

"Actually, I'm a firm believer in the family and in marriage. But I look at this as helping the marriage. I don't see it as a threat because I'm committed to my marriage and my family.

"If I discovered my husband had a lover, I wouldn't break up the marriage either. Even if my husband has had affairs, he's still an excellent husband, an excellent father, and his major commitment is to us. It's very naive to think there's no other person on earth who would ever appeal to a husband or wife.

"Here is this brilliant man Edward who wants *me*. I wouldn't give up the financial security of marriage or change my lifestyle. I enjoy traveling, theater, opera; I can enjoy Edward, too.

"Only a woman of a certain economic level can afford to have this kind of love affair. Every time I go to Washington, the plane fare alone costs me $200. I pay my own way, and I fly first class. It takes a certain amount of money to handle that. Once I flew up to Boston and back just for the day. $170. With cabs, it can run into money, so you have to be able to afford it. Domestic flights are cheap compared to a flight to Paris or Rome or Tel Aviv. But I have just lived that kind of life where I can travel and say it's on business. If anyone saw me in another place with another person, they wouldn't be shocked. Then there are the long distance phone calls which can be expensive. It costs me something. But we don't exchange gifts, nothing whatsoever. Once when we came back on the same plane to New York, he paid for his plane ticket with American Express and he said, 'Do you want me to take care of your ticket?' and I said, 'No, I have the cash.' I've been very independent about the whole thing, though he can well afford it. It's not just sex, it's friendship.

"My sex drive is not that high. With my husband, twice a month is fine. And when he travels . . . I don't know . . . I don't say I can't wait till my husband comes home, like some women. No, I don't have that kind of sex drive. I could certainly go four weeks without sex. So sex is not my frustration.

"But with Edward I enjoy sex. Oral sex, too. I like the licking which my husband doesn't do. I love the touching and the talking as much as the sex. There's a shyness about sex that's hard to change after 20 years. A certain pattern is established. It's much easier to start with someone new. Right from the beginning, the relationship is considered a purely sexual thing, so you can experiment. I have to be fair. It's easier to solve the marital crisis by having a lover than trying to fix up the relationship with your husband. I don't know if it's laziness, or shyness, or the fact that I don't think of my husband in sexual terms. Maybe it's a combination of all three.

"Even with everything I have, it isn't enough. I was always a high sensation person. I'm not willing to settle for what most people do. I need a lot of variety in my life. Maybe it's a certain greediness. I wonder what would have happened if I married

144

somebody with no money and my life was the supermarket and a struggle every day, and I couldn't go to the theater. A lot of people live that way. I don't think I would survive.

"I work. I entertain a lot. I have a lot of friends. I have pretty clothes and jewelry and all that. But I need a lot of different experiences. If I had to choose between having things and having experiences, I'd choose experiences any day. On the other hand, I realize I could not have these experiences without a certain amount of money.

"This affair with Edward is part of my life now—a very important part. I assume I'm not the only woman in his life, but I don't dwell on it. If he said it was over, I'd be very unhappy.

"A great many women want to have an affair. I think they're looking. It's only the opportunity they lack. If they're not working and meeting men, who is there? Unless they start up with their friends' husbands, there's not an available supply of men out there for women over 40. A lot is chance and luck. A few friends have told me that they wish they had a lover. Of course, I never say a word about myself. I've told my sister and two friends, that's all. Besides, most people see me as a very strongly married person. I can talk to my sister because she's not judgmental and she even likes my husband."

> She is earnest. She wants me to get the facts straight and interjects several times, "You understand? You see what I mean?"

"I don't believe in serial marriages. I don't believe in breaking up because of a sexual interest in someone else. I'm not going to sacrifice my marriage over this affair. No, I knew that right from the beginning, in my mid-thirties. First I said, 'Oh my God, what am I doing?' Then I got cooler, and I could see it very clearly as an extra.

"Right now I feel satisfied with things as they are. I'm not looking for someone who is very unhappily married and wants to attach himself to me. That's too much complication. Edward makes very few demands on me. He fits in very well with my life.

"Even if my daughter found out . . . She's 20 now and a sophisticated girl. When her boyfriend discovered that each of his parents were having affairs, she told him, 'What's so shocking? A lot of people do.' I could be open with my daughter and explain that it doesn't threaten my marriage. She'd understand.

"This is going to happen more often as more women go to work. It's a very European attitude—to have a lover, but preserve the marriage. Divorce and remarriage don't solve anything, do they? People get hurt, children suffer, and it's so . . . childish. I believe in the European way.

"Women can have it both ways. Definitely. But it takes a certain type of woman with a sense of logic, a woman who won't throw everything over for her lover. You have to know how to keep cool to handle both men. You need a lot of energy, and before you start you need a firm idea of how much you're willing to give and of what you're not going to sacrifice. You have to be able to lie a little, to be guiltless. You have to have the sort of personality that allows you to manage both the husband and the lover so the marriage isn't hurt.

"I have that ability. Some people couldn't handle it, but I can."

✲   ✲   ✲

Gina's story gives ample evidence of the many crises that confront married people in their thirties and forties.

Like Gina, many wives are faced with stressful periods. They discover a husband's affair, suffer profound disappointment in their children or their career, or find the marriage threatened by a serious illness. Sometimes it seems too much to bear.

Most wives cope with each problem as it comes up. Others cannot. They respond by turning to alcohol, or they break down physically or emotionally. They begin divorce proceedings, or, when they can't face the music, they run. The numbers of runaway wives have become an astonishing statistic in the last decade.

Or they may, like Gina, opt to continue the marriage and take a lover "on the side." They see him—as Ada described Larry—as "an oasis" from the painful situation at home.

For working wives, the burdens can become overwhelming. Unlike Gina, few families have the money to pay full-time housekeepers, so the problems of two-career couples are difficult ones.

William and Ruth Jones' book *Two Careers–One Marriage* discusses the extra stress and provides some guidance about dealing with it.

Working wives feel daily pressures to please the boss, to do a good job, and to move up—all the strains men feel at their jobs. There are household problems and the responsibilities of raising children. Even in egalitarian homes where husbands share the household work, it is generally the wife's responsibility to cover all the bases. The husband usually "chips in" or "helps her out." But if the husband is busy or absent, like Gina's, they wind up exhausted and resentful.

Women entered the work force in unprecedented numbers during the 1970s. Currently more wives are working (51 percent) than not working, which means that the demands on the family have changed considerably. Over 40 percent of women with preschoolers have jobs—6 million working mothers have children under six.* However, the gap in earnings between men and women has actually increased, and the situation of ordinary working women has not improved drastically. Susan Jacoby writes in *The New York Times*,† "There is little difference between sanitation workers and waitresses in education and training." But sanitation workers are men, they make much more, and they are represented by a union.

A television jingle for Enjoli perfume went like this: "I can put the wash on the line/feed the kids/Get dressed, pass out the kisses/ And get to work by five to 9/Cause I'm a woman." Most working wives are struggling to be superwomen. No wonder they're always tired.

A restaurant hostess and working mother says she is constantly running a marathon. "From the minute I bolt out of bed in the morning at 6:10, I'm on a split-second schedule. I slap together two sandwiches for the kids' lunch, pour cold cereal, and pop toast, plait braids, tie ribbons, and we're off. Music lessons? Brownie

* *Newsweek*, May 19, 1980.
† August 21, 1980.

Troops? Forget it. I squeeze in what I can for the kids. It's a struggle but who can stay home in 18 percent inflation. That's a luxury!"

The woman executive, with or without children, has other problems. Some of these women are choosing careers over motherhood, and some have put motherhood on hold for so long that the biological clock is running out. Competition between an executive wife and her husband can be keenly felt. Is she moving up faster than he? Are her salary and position outstripping his? Does he resent her success? Two high-powered executives under one roof can cause a crisis. Often their working schedules don't allow them enough time together. She's preoccupied with her work, and he with his.

"Sometimes my husband and I have to make an appointment to see each other. If I have to fly to the coast and he has a seminar to set up in Atlanta, we can go a week without seeing each other. There's simply not time, so he leaves a message on my answering machine and I leave a message on his machine. Is this any way to run a marriage? Sex? There's no time for real intimacy. With both of us keeping on top of our careers, our lives are getting busier and busier.

"It's ironic to think how carefully we used to plan time together when we first got married. We took long walks together. We'd spend a whole Sunday in bed. But with my career going full tilt and his promotion to Senior Lending Officer, we're ships that pass in the night.

"Before we made it careerwise, we had time to be crazy kids, to take a bath together, to do funky things. We once bought body paint and smeared designs all over each other. It was such fun. Crazy, erotic, and we laughed and laughed. But the job pressures are our number one priority now. And the only time we can be carefree is on a vacation. We're trying to schedule one now, and it's crisis time again. He has two weeks in May coming up, but I can't get away until the film is in the can. September maybe."

A mid-life crisis that comes to all couples—to working and non-working wives alike—is sexual boredom. Most couples are distressed to discover their passions have cooled. It is in the critical thirties that many wives look for devices to rekindle their husband's and their own interest in marital sex. They are at a stage when they may be feeling very sexy—but not about the man they've been sleeping with for ten or fifteen years. Some wives try to put excitement into the marital bed via a weekend away, a black negligee, a new position. The novelty may work to keep sexual boredom at bay, but all devices eventually lose their novelty. So, like Carol, they may decide that only another partner can reawaken them. Perhaps they flirt with another man at a party. It's a way of testing their powers. And sometimes they take this flurry of excitement home to be satisfied by their husbands. It feels so good to be aroused, even if the arousal was triggered by someone else.

Another device couples use to arouse themselves is fantasy, Nancy Friday's *My Secret Garden* documents a collection of women's secret erotic fantasies. One common fantasy wives use in the marital bed is that their partner is not Harry, that dull man they've been sleeping with for fourteen years, but Robert Redford or the cute guy they met at the party. Sometimes it works. And sometimes wives feel faintly guilty over it.

When all else fails to stimulate interest, some married women simply give up on sex. They become celibate—which obviously stretches their marital alienation further. Some couples use crises to build barriers between them. They bicker, snarl, and eventually fight openly as a method of avoiding sex. Even if there is no issue to quarrel over, they may invent one, purposefully picking a fight to get out of having sex. Dr. Theodore I. Rubin, when asked, "Is a woman's approach to sex any healthier than a man's?" answers, "Not healthier necessarily, but better integrated. If a man and a woman have a fight, for instance, and both are angry, the man can have sex and . . . go right on being angry . . . (but) if a woman is angry she's not likely to feel affectionate or aroused. . . . For most women sex is permissible as an expression of love."*

Many men over forty continue to have difficulty with the whore/madonna complex driven home to them when they were growing

* In *Harper's Bazaar*, March 1977, page 94.

up. They put their wives on pedestals—just as Gina's husband did—and introduce nothing more experimental than the missionary position with the lights out. Experimental sex they could pick up on a convention weekend.

Wives trapped into such patterns may experiment with their lovers. Oral sex—a *no-no* in the marital bed—turns out to be a wonderful turn-on with their lover. Hilma Wolitzer writes: "It seemed strange that I could do all those things with him, discover all those sensations and odors and that new voice that came from the dark pit of my throat (*Don't—oh, yes, oh God*) and that my mother and grandmother didn't know."* Experimental sex with a lover widens the gap between married and illicit lovemaking.

Yet, a wife can be turned off by her husband's insistence on experimentation. Betty was appalled when her husband brought home pornographic material to stimulate them. Donna became physically ill when her husband insisted on wife swapping with another couple. For many, sex starts in the head—between the ears, not between the legs. How they think about it stimulates or impedes them. Nancy Friday's *My Secret Garden* on fantasies may be stimulating for some, and for others, filthy pornography.

It is impossible to eliminate jealousy from marriage. Jealousy is a crisis that almost always occurs. Dory Previn says that men wander and women weep, that women worry while men are asleep.† The exclusivity contract of the wedding vows—"forsaking all others"—is a serious one for most husbands and wives. A sexual indiscretion can cripple a marriage, despite all the theory, rationalizations, and political statements to the contrary.

But there is a difference between a man's attitude and a woman's. "A man is worried about his wife going to bed with another man, a woman about her husband falling in love with someone else."‡ For many women penis-into-vagina is not the ultimate betrayal. It is the loss of love that hurts. The absence of sex in Ellen's

---

* In "Waiting for Daddy," *Esquire,* July 1971, Wolitzer describes a high school girl's early encounter with her boyfriend Arnie, which represented forbidden sex to her.

† Dory Previn, "Men Wander," 1971.

‡ Uta West, "If Love Is the Answer, What Is the Question?" page 116.

first affair with her spiritual lover didn't lessen the effect it had on her marriage. But the discovery that her husband was in love with another woman was far more shattering.

Jealousy is not limited to a sexual contender. It may come as a crisis over a friend or a child. Many husbands experience jealousy when the first baby is born. Sharing his wife's time and affection with the little intruder often triggers feelings of jealousy.

For most fathers, this is a temporary condition. The jealousy passes, and the couple takes pride in their offspring. However, jealousy appears in other guises. For example, later in the marriage, when an adolescent daughter discovers her own sexuality, the mother may become jealous.

"I hated her," a woman pushing 50 told me. "I hated her fresh complexion and her tiny waist and mostly her flat belly. She could get out of the house in the morning in twelve minutes flat and look delicious—while I was struggling with concealer under my eyes and control top pantyhose. What really turned me green was when Sam brought her presents and she cozied up to her Daddy and flirted. He just loved it. And I thought . . . he used to buy *me* presents. I was jealous. I knew it. Isn't that terrible? Jealous of my own daughter."

Raising children has, of course, always been a source of crises. School failures, drugs, alcohol, delinquency, and college tuition can strain the marriage severely. If the couple puts their children's needs first, that can easily erase the parents' relationship as romantic lovers.

"One year we had three kids in college at the same time. Three tuitions plus airline tickets, phone calls, and everything else. I worked two jobs, and Harriet worked full time, too. All we talked about was the kids. Which kids needed what? Which bill to pay? How to apply for a college loan? For our anniversary we took an overnight at the shore. It was a flop. Two ridiculous tired parents trying to be lovers again."

This is what Gina complained about—the responsibilities with which she was saddled and the resentments that built up.

When parents disagree over how to handle their children, rifts can develop that further strain the marriage.

"Henry wouldn't believe our son was into drugs. I was afraid to tell him. I couldn't face another crisis. I just put my head down on the kitchen table and cried."

Teenage pregnancy and abortion now loom as major problems. When a 35-year-old wife-turned-grandmother is forced to raise her grandchild, there is bound to be anger, resentment, and hostility. Arranging for a child's abortion is no less traumatic.

"If Tom ever found out Maryanne was pregnant, he would have gone crazy. She was only fifteen, a baby herself. She made me swear I wouldn't tell her father, and I had to arrange the whole abortion on the sly. It was the right decision. But I blamed myself. I should have been a better mother. It was my fault."

Few women over fifty take a lover for the first time. Opportunities decrease rapidly, and if monogamy has been a life pattern, it's hard to break at a late age. A woman past fifty may continue an established affair or begin a new one if she has had at least one affair in her thirties or forties. But the long-faithful wife who suddenly breaks out after fifty is an exception.

Many women refuse to consider menopause a crisis in their lives, to equate loss of reproductive power with loss of their sexual selves. Indeed, they may feel sexually freer, no longer concerned about pregnancy and at leisure to focus on themselves. Many discover energy they didn't know they had during the crisis-filled years of their thirties and forties. They also find renewed sexual pleasure within the marriage. In their book *Sex After Sixty*, Dr. Robert N. Butler and Myrna I. Lewis give specific recommendations for enhancing sexuality. If the passage of the years isn't turned into a continuing trauma, and if good health continues, a woman's sexuality can be heightened.

Gail Sheehy's book *Passages* is subtitled *Predictable Crises of Adult Life*. To understand that crises *are* predictable may take some of the sting out of them. "It would be surprising if we didn't experience some pain as we leave the familiarity of one adult stage for the uncertainty of the next," Sheehy says.

Each stage of life deals out many hands of cards. It's unlikely that among them there won't be some crisis to play out and face up to. A married woman who successfully handles crises is less likely to take a lover. Less tired, less frustrated, less disappointed in marriage, she is more likely to remain faithful. But if a wife cannot resolve the crises in her marriage, she may have a powerful motivation to seek comfort elsewhere.

CHANGING NEEDS: HELEN

WHEN STEPHANIE MET Roger at 24, she was a college dropout. He was graduating from medical school. She felt grateful to him for rescuing her from her "aimless life." She liked the routine of marriage and her part-time job as an advertising trainee. The first few years passed compatibly, until Stephanie got promoted to a full-time job. Longer hours and pressures to produce made her work late into the night at home.

"I resented waiting for her to come to bed," Roger said. "She used to be eager for sex. We'd start out fooling around on the sofa while we were watching television, and we could hardly tear our clothes off fast enough. Now I felt like a fool, pretending I was reading, waiting for my wife to come to bed. I had to be up at the crack of 6:15.

"But to hear her tell it, *I* was the monster. She started sniping that I should do the food shopping, take turns doing laundry and housework. She made demands and complained I was trying to hold her back. I thought I married a girl who appreciated me, not some flaming feminist with her damn equal rights talk. You know what did it? Her job. It turned the marriage sour."

Roger's analysis of what changed his marriage sounds believable, but let's let Stephanie tell her side of the story.

155

Having It Both Ways

"It wasn't the job that changed our relationship. It was me; I grew up. In the seventies, I was a teenage hippie without any purpose. My parents loved me, but they were too scared or too busy to cross me. So they let me do pretty much what I pleased, and they looked the other way when I did drugs or tanked up on beer. They were into their own lives, both successful establishment people and maybe I was an embarrassment to them. Anyhow, I drifted from one odd job to another, traveled and dropped out of college.

"Then I met Roger. We lived together, and I liked taking care of him. It gave me something to do. When he graduated and we moved back to Jersey, we did the wedding bit, and I got this little part-time job. My bosses liked me and put me on full time with a few lightweight clients of my own. I got substantial raises, and the pressure to produce forced me to take work home.

"But it wasn't the job that changed the marriage. It was *me*. I grew up. I got a sense of myself as a person. Now *I* want to achieve something. I want success on my own. I love Roger, and I want him to see the new me. My values are different, and my needs have changed. I'm not a kid anymore. I'm an adult and I like it that way.

"Roger says I turned tough. No, I didn't turn tough. I'm a woman now, and Roger can't hold on to the girl that he married. I can't be 'as soft and as pink as a nursery' like the song says, because I've changed inside."

It is not always an *outside* event that forces a woman to respond. The situation that looms as a crisis may come from *inside* her. *She* has changed. She has grown, she has matured, she has reevaluated her priorities. What pleased her, even delighted her at 21—"He was a marvelous dancer"—now bores her. What she thought "cute" is now irritating. What has changed? *She* has. The little girl has become a woman. Her *changing needs* now force her to reevaluate her marriage. And she doesn't like what she sees. The marriage needs an overhaul.

In their twenties, many young wives start out starry eyed, content to be somebody's wife and eager to be anything their husbands want them to be. To fulfill *his* dream is more than enough for them. But girls grow up into adult women. They find their own dreams as Stephanie did. Sometimes those dreams include a lover.

The trouble starts when one partner's growth does not keep pace with the other's. When one leaps forward and the other lags behind, the marriage gets out of sync. The brilliant professor at 42 is no longer the pimple-faced, yearning adolescent bridegroom. The 40 year old mother of three and owner of a boutique is no longer the unsophisticated, frightened bride. They are different people. Their aspirations, their dreams, their values have changed. They feel differently about the world. They feel differently about each other.

Jane married at 17 with stars in her eyes. She had a baby in nine months, and then another: "I was miserable—emotionally, financially, in every way." Once Jane revised her dream, she could not stay with her first husband.

Betty recounts the changes that occurred inside her—changes her first husband wasn't aware of. "I needed to know that I wasn't just someone's wife and mother of their children."

Betty's story is common among girls who come into marriage with a set of expectations and change along the way. In Betty's marriage it was the wife who changed. But just as often it is the husband who outgrows the wife.

There are women who marry and enter a world of chauffeuring kids, playing bridge, and doing volunteer work. In the meantime, their husband is constantly meeting new people, becoming involved in new projects and ideas. So the marriage suffers.

However, men can stagnate, too. If they come home, as Ellen's husband did, and watch cowboy movies on television, while the woman is evolving, she can outdistance him.

Under the old rules, husbands and wives accepted out-of-sync marriages. But younger couples have higher expectations.

Catherine, a 36-year-old mother of two, says the biggest change that occurred in her marriage is that she stopped saying, "I'm sorry." "When I was 21 and single, working as a secretary, I'd fall to pieces if I made a mistake. The *only* response I knew was to say 'I'm sorry, I'm sorry.' Right off, I'd apologize and accept the blame. If my boss said something was wrong, I crumbled. If the work was wrong, I was wrong. If the letter was bad, I was bad.

"Well, I took that same attitude into marriage, always apologizing. For the burnt toast. For a hole in my husband's sock. For whatever he complained about. I wanted to be a wonderful mother and homemaker—the perfect helpmate. So I was always on the defensive. Well, I changed. I grew up. Now when my husband or boss says something's wrong, I don't blame myself.'

This woman's opinion of herself changed as is sometimes the case when people "grow up."

Gail's story about her ex-husband shows how the change in her snapped the marriage.

"Christ, when I think what kind of shit I used to take from my first husband, I wonder why I let it go on so long. If he didn't like the way his shirts were ironed or I picked up the wrong beer at the liquor store, he'd wade into me like I committed a crime. Even slapped me around a couple of times, and it always wound up that I'd say that I was wrong.° You know why? I made him think he was God. I created him. I told him how wonderful he was, even when he abused me. I wanted to be nice, I was brought up to be nice. I wanted him to love me. I felt it was my place to soothe him and fix up his disappointments. So for years I took the shit he dished out.

"But then I had a disappointment, a deep disappointment. When I went to him for a little sympathy, all I got was, 'So what? Quit griping, I'm tired.' I was furious. Where the hell was he when I was down? I fed that man's ego for years. I figured I deserved something in return. Wasn't my disappointment worth anything?

"That's when it all changed for me. Something snapped. All those years I told myself I was happy. Well, that was the moment of truth. I talked back to that man. He called me a ballsy bitch and slapped me. I hit him back, and he slapped me again harder.° And I said: 'Bastard! You ever lay a hand on me again, and I'll call the cops on you. I'll put you away.' Inside I was shaking. But I stood up to him."

Gail's marriage ended in divorce. Her attitudes had changed.

Compliant women who become assertive women often are dis-

°*Sweetsir,* by Helen Yglesias, describes a similar marriage in which an abusive husband is killed by his wife.

°Maria Roy's book *Battered Women* deals with this subject. It is a psychological study of domestic violence which examines wifebeating and the role of alcoholism, drugs, and sexual and financial problems that precipitate assault.

paraged when they refuse to accept the treatment they accepted when they were first married: name-calling, abusive behavior, or physical punishment. The marriage deteriorates.

In the early years of marriage, couples set up rules. Whatever agreements they establish, most honor them. But when one partner changes the rules, it calls for a readjustment.

Susan Cohen's book *The Liberated Couple* describes some of the rules that change when a couple grows up.

"Early in her marriage, she was down on her knees scrubbing the floor when her oafish husband trampled across it in his muddy boots. She cried; he laughed, pointing out how trivial it is to cry over washing the floor. She pointed out to him that he wouldn't have laughed if he'd had to do the work over. No, indeed, he wouldn't have, would he? But she scrubbed it again."*

In one of his divorce cases, Chicago lawyer Michael Minton cited the wage value of a homemaker to be $793.79 a week, or $41,117.08 a year.† Most wives provide homemaker services free. Perhaps a more realistic figure is the one Jane O'Reilly, author of *The Girl I Left Behind*, uses. If the average suburban housewife were paid the federal minimum wage, it would cost her husband $16,000 a year, she says.‡

Liberated couples married in the seventies have less hassle over sharing household chores. It is generally long-married couples, whose work roles are traditionally sex-determined, who rebel over changing the rules. A wife who was taught to stand by her husband, to be at his beck and call, and to overlook what she didn't like, finds it hard to change the rules.

A successful writer who worked her way up through fifteen years of rejection slips told me how she labored on the kitchen table after she put the kids to bed.

"For years I allowed myself to write only after everything else was done. I'd bathe the kids, put them to bed, wash the dishes and clean up the kitchen, and work till my eyes got bleary. My husband

---

*Page 125.
†According to "Hot Line News" published by *Women U.S.A.*, 76 Beaver St., New York, New York. August, 1980.
‡According to John Leonard in *The New York Times*, September 29. 1980, p. C16.

would be watching a late show, and I'd shut the door. He viewed my efforts with a kind of amusement. He didn't take me seriously.

"Even when I had some success and my stories were included in anthologies, he continued to feel his work was more important than mine. After all, he was a successful stockbroker, he dealt with large money transactions. What did I make? $200? $300 for reprint rights? It didn't impress him.

"Until *I* changed the rules. 'I need a room of my own,' I told him. 'I can't go on working on the kitchen table.' He was surprised, but I persisted. 'I need a place to spread out, to keep my books. I need a file cabinet. I need a good light. I need a new typewriter.' I was full of *I needs*, me who never needed anything for herself, who always put him and the kids first.

"At first, he didn't know how to take it. But basically he's a good man, he's flexible and smart. He recognized the intensity in my voice. He set up a quiet place for me in the basement—a little room next to the washing machine. I love it. Finally I got a room of my own. Mine, all mine. I could be Virginia Woolf."*

Tillie Olsen's classic essay on writing, entitled "Silences," records the needs of women writers. "Substantial creative work demands time, undistracted time because when the responses come, availability to work is essential." Creative men knew this and protected their dreams by using their wives as buffers against the world.†　"Motherhood means being instantly interruptible, responsive, responsible. Children need one *now*," Olsen says.‡ This may be why creative women in the arts let *other* women be mothers. The difficulties of being an artist and a good mother are sometimes at odds.

Changing the rules in mid-stream can upset a marriage, whether it is the husband or the wife who initiates the change. One of those rules—perhaps the most hallowed—is the prohibition of extramarital affairs. Young, liberated husbands will sweep the floor, fold the laundry, and carry out the trash without flinching, but the husband who finds that his wife has a lover is generally so outraged, so

---

* Author of *A Room of One's Own*.
† See page 168 regarding playwright Eugene O'Neill's use of his wife.
‡ *Ms.*, September, 1978, page. 168.

horrified that his wife's affair—however meaningless or brief—can trigger the destruction of the marriage. Even avowed swingers in open marriage sometimes swing back to traditional restrictions on sexual freedom.

If women have changed the rules about their husbands, they have also changed the rules about their lovers. To be frightened little "back-street wives" waiting for the phone to ring is not their style. Of course, each love affair makes its own rules. The lovers work it out: where to meet; how often; when. But the woman who is balancing a life with a husband and a lover may make it clear she does *not* intend to give up her marriage. The lover must accept the rule that family comes first even if plans are canceled with the lover.

Another rule women make with their lovers is that when it's over, it's over. Gina's affair with Edward imposed those terms. She saw herself as a firm believer in the family and in marriage. The lover must understand that it will go on, even after the affair is over.

And finally, the lover must meet standards. Most wives who take lovers select thoughtfully. They hope for not only a sexual partner, but a friend who can offer stability, balance, and intimacy. An "erotic comradeship" is the phrase Barbara Deming uses in her book *We Cannot Live Without Our Lives.*

Many wives are independent women, whose rules now say they can leave lovers and not wait to be left. They accept parting as friends—no bitterness—each is free to go on and grow.

Helen, whom you will soon meet in this chapter, put a high priority on conversation and talking with her lover, as did Ellen and Fran. She considered it a big plus for her lover to be verbally expressive, as do many women today. A man must be sensitive and romantic, without clinging or making too many demands. Otherwise, a lover may turn into another husband. Gina said she would specifically exclude an affair with an unhappily married man.

As the rules change, women have changed their attitude about *women,* too. The old rule allowed a professional woman to be a snob about other women. Educated women felt women's conversations were beneath them, that it was men who really mattered.

That rule is fast changing. Women no longer feel women's talk is silly, trivial, and inferior to men's talk. They are showing new respect for other women, even less advantaged women not of their class and education. Women's issues are shared mutual concerns. They are less likely to accept being what Simone de Beauvoir called "The Second Sex."

A former dancer now in her sixties told me: "I used to shy away from women. I always preferred men's conversations. They seemed so much more lively and interesting. But things have changed. *I've* changed. I find women so much more interesting. I like women better."

All this reflects on their involvement with their husbands and lovers. Women who have strong ties with other women require less emotionally of their men, will not demand so urgently that their husband and/or lover furnish them with total emotional support. This can be good for a marriage.

Susan Jacoby writes: "In my experience, women do indeed make better friends for one another (and, for that matter, for men) than men do for one another (or for women)." While Jacoby fought an 18-month illness, her friendships—both male and female—were put to the test. Her conclusions? "Women were much readier to extend their tolerance than men. The men to whom I was closest tended to react either with open irritation or with cheerful reassurance about how good I looked."*

So women have not only changed in their relationships to husbands and lovers, but also to each other. And that, again, has changed their relationships with men.

Most wives who become mothers immerse themselves in that role. Playing house brings so much pleasure. Caring for their children makes their days so full that they hardly require "something extra" in their lives. It's enough to balance a husband, a career, a household, and a baby. Gail Sheehy says: "It is rarely possible for a woman to integrate marriage, career, and motherhood in her twenties, and it's about time some of us who tried it said so."† A lover would be a fifth wheel.

A wife who is going to stray will usually not look outside while she is still in her twenties. Through a decade of cooking and

New York Times column, "Hers," July 24, 1980.
†*Passages*, page 235.

washing and child-rearing—somehow, somewhere, she has displaced her Self. She tries hard to find herself under the demands everyone else makes on her. She's a wife, a mother, an employee, and often she puts her own needs last. Then one day she says, "Hold it! Wait a second. Who am I?—besides Janey's mommy and Bill's wife? Will I ever get past the next load of laundry?" The identity crisis strikes.

In her thirties, domestic resentments can build up. She stops and takes stock. Will she ever achieve what she wanted for herself? If she turned her happiness over to her husband during her twenties, in her thirties she is likely to blame him for not making her happy. If she put off a career or interrupted a flowering one to have children, she is likely to feel resentment. She picks her head up from the pile of dirty dishes in the sink and does a fast survey of her graduating class. Good God, look at her friends: three of them leading glamorous lives. Janice just published her first novel. Laurie is a top fashion designer. And Karen is a housewares buyer and travels to Europe twice a year. I was smarter than they, she thinks. *How the hell did I end up with a sink full of dirty dishes?*

In her thirties or forties, a wife may feel the bottom falling out. Something's gone sour. Her husband is a nice guy, but he's changed. He's not romantic, he's not sexy anymore. He's too busy earning a living. He takes it all for granted—the Thanksgiving dinner she once loved spending four days preparing, the baby's birthday party with 22 mommies and their kids. Who now carries the heavy burden of responsibility?

She takes inventory. Even if her household is well-run, even if her children are fine, if her career is satisfying—there comes a time when the dream looks tarnished. It's not enough. *Nothing's enough.* The theme is a recurring one.

"I no longer felt it was up to Ken to make me happy. I felt it was up to me," a 38-year-old mother of two said. "Look, you grow a new layer of skin, right? Your cells are replaced, your hair, your fingernails get new growth every day. Why not a new person? I found this new person inside me. And Ken didn't see it. To him I was still a giggling little bride who blushed if someone said *shit.*

"Although Ken didn't see it, Leo did. Nothing was lost on Leo. He listened to me when I talked, really listened. And you know what he said? I'm the first investment analyst he met with a sharp, logical mind. That I'm gonna have a seat on the Exchange before I'm 40. Now that's a dream I can buy!'

A 41-year-old teacher of the blind said: "What I wanted when I was 22 was a good provider. I got my dream. What I wanted was a tough, macho guy. I admit it, that turned me on. I liked the way my husband made all our decisions. He was The Man, and he told me what to do.

"But I'm 41 now and I don't like it anymore. I've changed. My lover is the opposite. He's soft and tender and he talks about things my husband wouldn't understand. Vic sees a side of me my husband doesn't know—the other person, the secret person I really am. I tell Vic my dreams and he tells me his."

When the dream changes in mid-life, everything seems to change along with it.

"The change came over me when I was 39," a 46-year-old programmer for a cable television company said. "I was working for a bank at the time and they were willing to pay for my M.B.A. My husband was all for it. Free tuition and a raise was all he could see. What he didn't see was the new person I was. I became competitive, I wanted more. I wanted to move up.

"Hal was in my accounting class. We became friends. Then lovers. He put me on to this job in cable television. I started out selling time, worked into advertising manager, and now I'm Director of Program Development.

"My husband? He's still a furniture salesman, counting the days to retirement. Me? I feel like 30. I'm just starting out."

Dorene and Marsha, two mid-forties women, tell a different story of how their husbands helped them start their own business when their dreams changed. "Our friends were feeling the empty-nest syndrome. Their kids were gone and they were restless. Marsha was my best friend and we talked about going back to work, but we were always waiting for the right moment.

"Anyhow we took an arts and crafts course, and a boutique paid us $35 for our ceramic flower arrangement. We started taking orders, and in two years we became entrepreneurs of *Mar-lene's Party Goods*.

"We couldn't have done it without our husbands' support. They helped us with money, they put up fixtures, and they gave us encouragement. They said: 'If that's your dream, do it!'"

164

Like Dorene and Marsha, wives often reach out to their husbands first. Does he see the new person she has become? Does he encourage her dream? A wife who's disappointed in her husband is more likely to look elsewhere.

"Getting involved with a lover was the farthest thing from my mind. But I was overpoweringly attracted to Michael. I was feeling scared at the time and he made me feel capable. At 38 I was lovesick. Married 18 years and in love with another guy. I didn't want the affair, I didn't go out looking for it. But something happened to me at 38. I took stock of my life and revised my dreams and I decided to take drastic action.

"Why settle when I could improve my lot? My friends were flocking to psychiatrists. They felt helpless and depressed. Why pay a psychiatrist? A lover did more for me. My husband and I shared nothing anymore. He was in his world and I was in mine. But Michael—well, I'm a new person with Michael."

There comes a time when a woman's husband may have lost his magical powers over her. She's no longer afraid of him, in awe of him, or dependent on him. She revises her dream.

Or quite the opposite, perhaps her friends are divorcing right and left, and she's afraid of being left for a younger woman. She wants only to please him. *So she revises her dream.* Whatever her dream may have been earlier, many a wife rewrites the script in her thirties and forties. Some wives feel suddenly competitive, anxious to find new mountains to climb. Others feel fed up with the rat race and happy to explore their nurturing and creative sides, eager to have a baby, stay home, and sew curtains. Whatever the earlier dream, it suddenly seems outdated.

"When we were first married, I was willing to accept my husband's dominance," a doctor's wife told me. "he made the money, big money, and he was the kingpin. I was busy raising kids and with half my friends divorcing, I was afraid my marriage could be the next to go. I was scared to be demanding. But deep down I hated him for the power he had over me. He held the pursestrings, and I had to come to him for every cent. Me—a Phi Beta Kappa with a master's in art history. It rankled.

"Then two years ago when I turned 44, I got a job teaching a course in college. I didn't tell him, and I opened a savings account. Through a fluke, I got a full-time appointment to $12,000 a year and

I realized he had no more control over me. I could support myself and I got Blue Cross, Blue Shield, life insurance, and a pension plan. I bought my own car. And for the first time in my whole life, I feel I'm in charge of my life. I picked up a lover along the way. Allan was one of my students, a police officer who returned for his master's. How do I feel? On top of the world!"

Wives dominated by benevolent dictator husbands may sit out their hostility for years. But once they revise their dream, husbands lose power over them. In Lois Gould's novel *Final Analysis*, a woman says: "The only reason I hated him was that I had needed him so much. That's when I found out about need. It goes much better with hate than with love."

A young executive husband just starting out may have no problem with an unsophisticated wife. But when he becomes a tycoon, he may consider her a social handicap. The same may happen to a wife. At 20, she may be delighted to play her husband's devoted help-mate. But when she spreads her wings at 38 or 44, she'll resent anyone who tries to hold her down.

Carlotta Monterey O'Neill explained her relationship to her famous playwright husband:

"I had to work like a dog. I was Gene's secretary, I was his nurse. His health was always bad. I did everything. He wrote the plays, but I did everything else. I loved it. It was a privilege to live with him. . ."*

However, for a capable woman married to an ordinary man it's often frustrating to be left home with domestic chores while her husband is living the exciting life of travel and expense account restaurants. He seems to be the *bon vivant;* she feels that she is his slave.

"Until I was 33, I never asked for much," a 40-year-old hairdresser told me. "Then something changed: I demanded things I never before had the guts to ask for. First I told my husband I was joining a Tuesday bowling league with a girl from the shop. He was miffed, but I left him something in the refrigerator and went.

"The big change came later. When we went out together, I never used to express an opinion. He did all the talking. Well one night he

*Quoted in *O'Neill*, by Arthur and Barbara Gelb.

said something dumb while we were playing cards, four of us, and I disagreed with him. When we got home, he ordered me never to contradict him in public again. 'I didn't contradict you,' I said, 'I just stated my opinion. Aren't I entitled to my own opinion?' I thought he was going to haul off and smack me, he was so mad. 'You keep your big mouth shut!' he said. And I said, 'You can't stop me from talking. I'm a person!'"

For most wives changing from homemaking to career woman, the most critical factor is a husband who contributes practical and emotional support to his wife's success. When she walks down the aisle on graduation day, he crows. He encourages her and enjoys her new friends. But if a husband puts obstacles in his wife's path, if he won't agree to her changing demands, the marriage can run into difficulty.

New demands can include time for herself.

"When I told Rob I wanted a weekend away by myself, he went up in smoke. 'Are you crazy?' he said. All I wanted was one lousy weekend, two days to go skiing, and he hated cold weather. But he put up such a fuss. 'We never go on separate vacations. What are you asking for? You can't change the rules!'"

"Well, I did. And he got over it. Now when I need time off, he doesn't put me through hell. He seems to understand and it makes our vacations together more valuable."

A weekend off is not a major rewrite of the marital rules. But a decision to have a baby is—if the couple has agreed to remain childless.

"We're both successful career people with an active social life, and we planned to keep it that way. But then, around 36, I began to feel maybe the clock was running out for me. I wanted to have a baby. My husband said no, kids are problems, they hold you down. He was angry that I was making unreasonable demands.

"But I was getting panicky. I read about women over 40 and abnormal births. Also, I was up for a full partnership. I'd wake up in a sweat at night wondering if I would make a good mother, or if we should put off the decision for another year. Was Simone de Beauvoir right—that maternity fulfills a woman's psychological destiny? I was obsessed with the Baby Problem. Was a baby an unreasonable demand?"

Having It Both Ways

*   *   *

When I interviewed Helen, her story documented many of the changes women experience in their thirties. In fact her interview— perhaps because she was an older woman in her sixties—touched many of the motivations we've seen in previous chapters: hostility to her husband; sexual problems; and lack of communication in the early years. Until she was 35, Helen responded by having casual affairs—short-term bandaid affairs. It wasn't until her mid-thirties that everything changed for her. She began an affair with "the love of my life," a man who was to become her lover for fifteen years.

I met Helen by contacting a chapter of the Gray Panthers, a group that works for the rights of older people. When I explained on the phone that I wanted to insert an ad in their newsletter to say: "Established author seeks women interviewees for important new book on married women with lovers," the ladylike voice at the other end hesitated a moment, then asked, "Would you like to *interview me?*"

Helen's three-room apartment was located in a cluster of brick garden apartments on a noisy, heavily trafficked intersection.

"Come in," she greeted me with a ready smile. "Please come in."

I entered a neat living room of Danish Modern furniture. A basket of shiny red apples and a tea-service were set out on the coffee table.

She had a sweet, unlined, pretty face, light brown eyes that were warm and twinkling, and a head of tousled, very white hair. She wore navy plaid slacks and a baby blue turtleneck sweater—a slim woman, clean-faced, friendly, and interested in this book.

We talked a little about her work in the Gray Panthers and fighting local neighborhood crime. She wanted older people to feel safe on the streets. She took buses to work every day to get to the computer company where she was a secretary.

She told me a friend of hers—also an older woman—had been mugged on the street, knocked down, and her purse stolen.

Helen had a soft and gentle manner, a hesitation of speech that suggested thoughtfulness, intelligence, and sincerity.

I set up the tape recorder on her coffee table beside the basket of apples and she poured us each a cup of tea.

Changing Needs: Helen

✿   ✿   ✿

"I was married at 21. At 23 I had my first affair.

"In my twenties, I took lovers casually. I needed something to compensate for the loneliness and emptiness I was finding in my marriage. But somewhere in my mid-thirties, my needs changed and I found I didn't want just a sex companion for a few hours. I wanted a loving relationship, a long-term lover-friend.

"When I was 35, I met the love of my life. It lasted a long time, until his death. I call fifteen years a long time, don't you? The last five years, because he moved out of state, it was mostly visits back and forth, and letters and phone calls. So I took another lover after Frank and that lasted ten years, but it's over. I have someone else now. I supose at my age—I'm past 60—it fills a sort of vanity, a need to know I'm still attractive to men. But then? I was unfaithful to my husband for a number of reasons. But to my two long-term lovers I was absolutely faithful.

"The man that I married was . . . well . . . ."

She sits thoughtfully, staring into space.

"I'm trying to find the right words. I want to get it right for you. The man I married felt a great need to fight the world. He made more enemies than friends. So this narrowed down our circle of acquaintances. Even members of the family dropped away, he was so unpleasant. Something impelled him to fight. I know what it was.

"He was the oldest of eight and when his family broke up, he was literally abandoned, thrown out by his father and mother. At 13 he was sleeping on stair landings, picking food out of garbage cans. He couldn't go to school, he had to find any kind of work to live. So he emerged very angry, hating everyone. And it spilled over into our relationship. He'd say, 'Don't talk to this one or that one,' and I was not permitted to talk to anyone. I got so lonely that out of desperation, I sought relationships he couldn't know about.

"I felt such anger toward him. I became cold and I refused sex. So he'd punish me. How? Withdrawal of money. When I refused sex and he was getting fed up waiting for me, he wouldn't give me

169

food money. I remember the third day I asked him for money and he would't answer me. I called a friend who lived across the city, and she said come right over. I pushed the baby's stroller 32 blocks so we could have a meal. And from that day on I learned to skim off a few dollars; everytime he gave me something I'd put a little aside. I learned how to make it vanish into a private little fund so that if anything happened, I'd have something. I learned that money is a weapon.

"Then there was his absolute silence. The anger was seething inside him. I tried a few times to be nice, but I didn't like myself for being nice. We got into a vicious cycle.

"The only way I could enjoy sex was outside the marriage. I remember one man asking, 'Why me?' And I said, 'Because we have no quarrel with each other.' He didn't understand. But for me it was a very satisfying answer.

"Being a social person, I liked to go out. In the beginning I was only looking for companionship and venting my hostility without wanting to break up the marriage. Then it got to be too much for me and I told him I wanted to end the marriage. But he cried and pleaded with me, 'Don't. If you have any loyalty and devotion you won't do that.' So I felt terribly guilty. Before the children came, I tried to break it up, but each time he'd cry and I'd go back.

"And then I'd have another little affair. It was the only moment I had away from his anger.

"But then when I was 35, everything changed.

"I had known Frank for years. He was a friend and he'd join us on outings with his wife and children. I had two little girls by then—nine and six—and he'd come along with us. Simple little things. A day on the beach, a ride in the car. He enjoyed children and the kids got a kick out of him. At that time I didn't think of him as somebody who would have a special part in my life.

"Then all a sudden, I began to think of him in a different perspective. I wanted to know him better than this superficial, pleasant relationship. And I told him. He answered me, 'If you hadn't spoken up, I would have.'

"From then on we entered into an intimate relationship. It was difficult at times, but very beautiful. For the first time I was in a really loving relationship. It was not like those other men—some orgasms and goodnight. This was completely different. It was a marriage within a marriage.

"Frank was 15 years older than me. He enjoyed people, he had a sense of humor and he always found something to be light about. It wasn't that he made jokes, but he brought a laugh to whatever we were talking about. He was fun to be with.

"In the beginning there were close calls. It was a matter of making time to be together and taking time off from work. We'd meet about twice a week. We couldn't always sleep together, so sometimes it was just being together, talking, walking, a cup of coffee together. Keeping in touch and maintaining an intimacy. It was an emotional bond we had. When I was 23 or 24, all I wanted was casual sex. But now it was different. I didn't want that anymore. I was mature, grown up, and I wanted an adult relationship.

"The first time I slept with Frank we went to a hotel. I remember I was about to take my dress off and he stopped me, He said, 'Don't rush. Please. I love you. This is just the start of a lifetime.' And that's how it was. Not like those early affairs. I was a mature woman now and it was more important to get to know each other. The getting into bed would come later. It did. And we had that intimacy for 15 years.

"How did I manage to keep it from my husband?"

She laughs, a twinkling merry laugh, and gets up to pour us another cup of tea. From the tiny step-in kitchen off the living room, I see her place fresh tea bags in our cups, as she calls to me, "With care. With great difficulty." Then she returns carrying two fresh cups of tea.

"There was a period when he suspected, but he didn't actually confront me. He did it in a roundabout way. I think he overheard a tone of voice in a phone conversation with Frank and he became very angry. He began to smash records. Then silence.

"Once he hit me, but it was in an earlier period before we had children. I told him I had somebody and I was leaving him. I felt rotten about it, I was crying, but I packed my bag and I was going to walk to the subway. He didn't say a word. He slapped me hard.

Then he picked up my bag and walked me to the subway. A week later, he came to me crying. It was the only time I admitted I had somebody else.

"In the early days, we'd arrange it by phone. He'd call me at work, and we were in touch almost every day. He lived nearby, and he was in a business similar to ours. By that time, my husband had a successful mail order business.

"Frank and I had an extremely strong relationship. A bond of love and sex and friendship. So strong, we decided to have a child together.

"We both wanted to have a child. And we did. He remained married, and I did too. But we had this lovely child. A little girl. Together. And the child gave us great joy.

"I remember he came to the hospital to visit. And we both looked at each other and enjoyed it tremendously. He always found time to come to us. To be with us. The first time I was able to take the baby with me after I had been discharged from the hospital, we met in a restaurant. I was holding her in my arms and the three of us sat there at the table in absolute contentment. I don't think we ate much. We were just so happy to be together. We felt like a family.

"Of course my husband thought the baby was his. He accepted her, and he made a good father to her. But Frank and I knew. She was our lovechild.

"She was not an error, not a mistake. It was planned. When Frank and I made the decision to have a baby together, we didn't consult anyone else. Of course there were doubts in our minds. But I didn't feel it would be a burden to my husband. We talked about how Frank would feel fathering a child he couldn't acknowledge. But he decided this was the way it had to be. There was no point in leaving our spouses. We each had two children. There was no reason to deliberately hurt them. We had no religious taboos, no religious backgrounds to interfere. There was just no reason to hurt everyone else.

"Of course we knew that if this became known it could destroy the relationship between us and our respective families. We wanted our families to be friendly and to continue to go out together. Frank's wife never suspected. And to this day, my younger daughter believes her father was my husband. As it turned out, he enjoyed having this third child. He got a great deal of pleasure out of her. She was a lovely child to raise. She had a serene disposition. She could hardly wait for him to come home at the end of the day. She was his little darling, she adored him. She'd start screaming with glee when he came home, and he'd sweep her up in his arms.

"This was no burden. And Frank wasn't jealous. This is the way it had to be. We both knew it.

"My husband was truly a good father to her. So I have no regrets about that decision. Not at all. It's one of the best things I ever did. It's funny . . ."

She chuckles at some long-forgotten memory that pleases her.

"My third daughter doesn't resemble either of us. Not Frank, not me. This little girl skipped both of us. She looks like my mother.

"She's 23 now. A bride herself. And she's a lovely human being. People like her. She's the kind that doesn't put on airs, you know? The older children never suspected. No one did. Though my children know today that I had lovers. They don't know who or when. And they shouldn't.

"Of course the whole time Frank and I were lovers, I was still sleeping with my husband. Sort of. But sex with him was rotten. He took his anger to bed with him. And as I began to withdraw sexually, he wanted more sex. More oral sex, any kind of sex. But I found sex with him awful. With Frank sex was always a happy, loving time. With my husband—well his frustrations over a wife who was turning colder and colder just made him want to have more to compensate for what he wasn't getting out of it.

"He was never satisfied. He wanted to have me suck him. He wanted it to take a long time, to make it linger. If I'd give up, he'd say, 'Keep it up, keep it up.' The same dialogue again and again. And frankly I was getting awfully tired. It could be a matter of hours, and I would be absolutely exhausted. Until finally, he came. It was so unpleasant.

"I don't know why I let the marriage go on. I used to feel I had no choice. I had two young children. Until I had children, I felt independent, I felt I could always pick up and go. But now I knew I was trapped. I didn't have that freedom. How was I going to make ends meet? I made one last attempt before I became pregnant with Frank's child. I tried to leave. But I came back. And I told him: 'This is tiring me out. Please. Let's find some middle ground. We have different needs about sex.' And he said: 'Okay. How long do you want me to wait? Three days? Four days? How long?' It didn't work. At the end of the time, there it was hanging over me. I had to perform again.

"He wanted to . . . I don't know the proper word for it . . . oral sex on a woman."

I supply the word, cunnilingus, and she nods.

"Sex with him was terrible, I didn't enjoy any of it. I knew he was going through hell too because he had difficulty coming. He'd ask me to masturbate him to climax, but nothing happened. And I was no longer even pretending to participate in this act.

"He wanted me to get dressed up in black lace underwear and to whip him. I just couldn't develop any enthusiasm for whipping. Not that I'm such a Puritan, but some things . . . I mean you experiment to find out what you like, but you draw the line. He wanted to urinate into my vagina. He wanted to urinate into my mouth, insisted on it. But there was no way he could force my head into that position. He tried to clamp his hands on my head, but I jerked out of his hands. It was impossible. I couldn't take it. he insisted I swallow his come. I gagged. he asked for anal sex, but on that one point he accepted my refusal because I had had surgery for hemorrhoids. Nothing worked. He brought home dirty pictures and he took me to a burlesque. Nothing. Because I didn't feel good towards this man.

"The greatest turn-on is the good emotions between two people. Between Frank and me there was love. That's all I needed. Love. It just enveloped me completely. The touching and the tenderness. The spontaneity about lovemaking. it wasn't programmed, not a routine like first you kiss the nipple, then you put your big toe there. It's a matter of feelings, see? What you feel about another human being.

"Frank was a loving and caring person. I remember one weekend we took off by ourselves. Just a Saturday and a Sunday, but it was lovely. We went out of town. We did a lot of walking and talking. Sightseeing, just looking around. Sharing thoughts. Being together with one another. Alone, intimate, in bed. And all the talking going on. We'd talk about our children, what we wanted out of life, about people in general, about the world situation. Everything. Frank was a wonderful talker.

"Sometimes I wondered why I ever married my husband.

"I met him on New Year's night, 1940. Maybe I saw something cleancut in him then. I remember how surprised he was when I said 'Dutch Treat' on our first date. I was working then and I didn't want to take advantage. I was independent, spirited, and I felt I should pay my own way. After we got married, I continued to work until I became a mother. Then I stayed home for a few months. However, that was shortlived because . . . . well this is how it happened.

"We tried to build a business together. From the kitchen table in our New York tenement. It was a direct mail business. And my husband suggested we reverse roles. He would stay home because he wanted to build the business. And he would take care of the baby who was about six weeks old. I'd go back to work. That was fine with me. It satisfied my need to be with people, and it turned out that he was a marvelous father. He enjoyed preparing the formula and feeding the baby, and the same thing happened when the second baby was born. I went back to work right away and he stayed home with the children.

"At first we had common goals, the things we wanted in life were pretty much the same. We hoped to leave New York and move to the suburbs. To give our children a better atmosphere. To enrich their lives with the things of the mind, rather than what money could buy.

"Little by little the business picked up. We were able to take it out of the tenement into a small loft. Then into a larger loft. And one day we had enough to buy a small house. I told the real estate agent in Connecticut that we wanted a house in an interracial neighborhood and that kind of stunned him. I guess he didn't know too many people with a social conscience. But going through the Depression made me feel strongly about poor people. I still feel that way. Some things never leave you, I guess.

Having It Both Ways

"I was raised by my mother. She and my father separated when I was quite young, and I didn't see my father for many years. Anyhow, the whole time I was growing up as a teenager, she'd say, 'When you grow up, don't get married.' She'd say it a lot. 'Don't get married.' It was an understandable attitude. Her marriage wasn't successful and she wanted me to have the freedom she didn't have. She was hoping I'd have a career, to prove that a woman could do what a man could do. She was a feminist in her day. In fact, I was born on a certain day when something special happened in American history. Something about the women's suffrage movement, and she called me her little suffragette.

"But when I was going out with my husband and I told her I wanted to live with him . . . to my absolute surprise . . . she turned to me and said, 'You must be sick!' It's funny. Theory and practice are two different things. When the time came, she reversed herself. So I got married. You know something? It would have been better if we'd lived together. Maybe it would have given us the necessary time to know each other. I only knew my husband two months.

"I think young people who live together until they decide to have a child have the right idea. My children know my feelings on this. The older two both got married conventionally. The oldest has a child, so I'm a grandmother now. But my youngest daughter was more influenced by my thinking. When she met the man she cared for, they lived together a year. You know what?"

She has a mischievous glint in her eye.

"They got married. Only a few months ago. Hard to believe. My lovechild is a married woman.

"With Frank lovemaking was a slow-growing thing. There was time to appreciate each other as people. Even before I was in love with Frank, I liked the way his mind worked. I liked his body. I liked . . . most of all liked *him*. It was the total human being. There were other bodies more attractive than Frank's, sure. But that didn't matter. He made me feel good. We made each other feel good just to be alive. Life was worth living because we had each other. As I fell more and more deeply in love with Frank, I withdrew more and more from the marriage.

"There was a change in me. One night we had a fight and my husband packed a bag and stayed away two days. I was worried. I didn't have a car, I couldn't drive. But I also discovered two things: First, I still had a fiercely independent nature in me. I still had enough fire to find a way to make ends meet. Second, I knew that I could take care of myself and my children. I didn't earn enough money, so I knew it would be a struggle. But I knew I would keep on trying.

"In New York there were day care centers, but out in the suburbs there was nothing. Anyhow, while I was mulling it all over, he came back. Full of regrets, with gifts for everyone, trying to make amends. I was now raising three children, living in a big house in the suburbs, and my whole life was running a different pattern. I was changing again and reestablishing my values. But sexually, it was the same old thing. I'd make excuses. He'd get upset and turn and toss all night. Eventually, we went to twin beds. But even then, you can't block out the tension in the room. You feel it, no matter what.

"Then one night . . ."

She hesitates and squints her eyes as if she's trying to get the picture in focus.

"One night, he went into the bedroom where my older daughter slept. He got into bed with her. She was about twelve. And she came running to me, 'Mommy, tell Daddy to get out of my bed. I can feel his penis.' I stormed in there and just gave it to him! At which point he packed his bags and left. Again. This time he was gone three weeks. But again, he came back, and again with presents. This happened periodically until just before the twenty-fifth anniversary.

"We were having a party. We were in the kitchen and I glanced outside at the guests. I said, 'Look. Look at them. We're miserable and our guests are down there in the pool having a ball. Let's end it.' 'No,' he said. 'Let's go away for a weekend to the mountains.' I said, 'No, let's go to a marriage counselor.' But he wouldn't go. And I wouldn't go on the weekend. So he went by himself. When he came back, he said, 'I saw so many lonely women out there. If our marriage breaks up, you'd be one of those women.' He was pleading with me to make a go of it. This time he went to a marriage counselor. But after two sessions, he was at odds with the therapist. There was an open confrontation. So at this point, at the 25-year mark, I told the children, 'The marriage is over.' The two older ones said, 'You should have done it a long time ago.' But the youngest one loved him and said she was going to miss her father.

"This time my mind was made up. Why did it take 25 years? We had made great financial strides by then. My husband was riding the crest of a wave of success. We were both able to enjoy the things money could buy. Unfortunately, we had lost sight of our goals. I didn't want to put money into fancy things that you wear on your back. I wanted the enrichments of life. That was my dream. But he became very materialistic because we had money. Being so successful, the business was no longer in the house. It was in a building, and it flourished. We moved to a larger house with a swimming pool. He had cabanas built, and we had everything. But the marriage wasn't good, and all that the money did was to buy temporary acquaintances. We entertained lavishly, invited people over, and played the genial hosts. But it was all very superficial. Our goals had changed. We had nothing in common.

"Even if I hadn't had Frank, the marriage wouldn't have survived. I was torn the whole time. Wanting to leave the marriage, wanting to be with Frank, knowing he wanted to be with me. We saw each other or we talked on the phone almost every day.

"Of course passion never stays at one level . it goes up and down. You change. You grow. Your values change. Your goals change. Mine did. But the good feeling I had with Frank remained constant. We were very much tuned in to each other. It was a pleasure to be together. That's the feeling that leads to good sex, and good sex is, after all, just another way of expressing your enjoyment. Holding each other's faces, cupping it like this."

She demonstrates, placing her face in her hands.

"That was sheer pleasure! So loving. Which led to the sensuous things. We showered together. Did you know it's easier to move around in a shower than a bathtub? We also experimented with different positions. We tried out fantasies. It was good between us.

"My husband remarried twice after our divorce. That got pretty

178

ugly. He used money against me again. Closed on the house, but wouldn't co-sign the check for the sale, so the money had to be held in escrow. I walked away without a cent. Just a very deliberate spiteful act. He died last week."

Did I hear her right? "Last week?" I repeat. I ask her if this is a difficult time to be going over it all.

"No, no, it's all right. He disowned all three children. When he felt his wisdom was in question, when they wanted to make decisions for themselves, he disowned them. Cut all three out of his life. When the youngest decided to live with her young man, he called her a whore. Hateful. He was full of hate. When the children were small he was a good father, an adoring daddy. But when they grew up and he was confronted with a full individual, the relationship was over. His second marriage lasted only a few months. The third a few years. He had no other children.

"I suppose my story says a married woman can have it both ways because I did. But if you mean can a woman be in control of both relationships—well, I haven't met such a woman. I was unfaithful for a number of reasons. In my twenties, casual sex was fine. Because I was angry, I was hostile, I felt cut off and lonely. But you change as you live. Whether a woman takes a lover to get even with her husband or to escape a crisis in her marriage or . . . well it changes all the time. Because *you* change, too.

"If one of my married daughters came to me for advice, I'd listen, that's all. I have no answers. I've had several love affairs. They seemed right for me at the time. But I don't like to think it proves that marriage is obsolete. I'd hate to see it disappear. There's something very comfortable about a long-term relationship.

"After Frank died, I took another lover. A much younger man, but that didn't bother me because my body was physically not aging yet and I tried to keep my mind bright and alert. I was 50, he was 30, with very young children. We had a relationship for over ten years. We still do. As friends. It was sexual for many, many years. But I knew his family and I felt guilty about his wife. I didn't want any harm to come to them, I like them too much. This is a man who will have women throughout his life, although he claims to love his wife. But he loves other women, too. Maybe men can do this. Love the wife, love the children, love the marriage. And still have another woman. But women? A woman can't do it as easily.

"Of course, as women go out and work, they come in contact with many men. Their lifestyles, their attitudes and values change. Having a lover can become a way of life. Some women are reacting to it the same as men. But I hope we don't imitate men's worst qualities.

"But we have our needs, too. So if we demand perfection and we don't get it, we look for compensations.

"There's one thing I do feel. When a woman takes a lover, the children suffer. They're losing part of the mother's concentration on her children. Her thoughts are divided. No matter how hard she tries, her thoughts are on her lover. And a child senses the vacant look in the mother's eye. While she's diapering the baby, she's wishing she were in her lover's arms. While she reads a bedtime story, she's planning her next meeting with her lover. It's draining. It's diverting. It takes attention and care away from the child. I felt no guilt about my husband. But I did feel guilty about the children.

"But children grow up. They need you less. So my priorities changed. I felt it was a matter of survival for me to have Frank. All those years when I was young I had men I didn't care about. I had sex without love, sure—you can have pure sex without love. Men can. And women can, too. But if you're fortunate enough to have sex with love that's the highest, that's the best.

"Last year I discovered I had cancer. It was removed and the surgeon told me I'm cured. But it made me stop and think and really take a look at my life. You know how I feel? I want to savor every day.

"The best part of having an affair is that it's fun. Fun! It makes you feel good to be alive."

❖　　❖　　❖

Sexual difficulties that remain unresolved from the early days of marriage sometimes seem suddenly to erupt beyond endurance. When a woman is experiencing other changes in her thirties and forties, those sexual difficulties can become unbearable. Perhaps, like Helen, a young wife puts up with it for the sake of the children. Perhaps she sees no other options or she may even keep hoping that things will improve. But all at once, nothing seems to help—not even a brief one-night stand here and there. It's not the sexual situation that has worsened. The woman herself is experiencing some real physical and emotional changes at this time. If marital sex now appears unbearable—and a number of other factors come together at this time—a wife may decide, as Helen did, to seek a love affair outside the marriage.

In her late thirties and early forties a woman reaches the peak of her sexual powers. This period often coincides with marital boredom. The disparity between male and female sexual appetites are most likely to be keenly felt now. Sexually, husbands and wives may become less and less synchronized. While many changes are taking place emotionally and psychologically, the most critical ones seem to manifest themselves in the bedroom. Biology supples an explanation. While a man is in his sexual prime around the age of 19, a woman's prime comes along about twenty years later, when her mate has slowed down. She may be feeling feverish, urged on by her appetites, but her rosy glow may not be for her husband.

"He got fat. He got bald. He got careless about cleanliness," a telephone operator said about her husband. "On the physical side he was a slob. But the rest was no better. He was angry—all the time angry. Nothing suited him. Everybody was his enemy, out to cheat him. How can you have sex with a man like that? He picks on you all day and expects you to fall into his arms at night. Well, I'd rather get in bed with a baboon."

When boredom, anger, and resentment pile up, when couples squabble all day, sexual passion is hardly going to flow at night. Masters and Johnson wrote: "Nothing good is going to happen in bed between a husband and a wife unless good things have been happening between them before they got into bed."* Because sex isn't a function separate and apart from their lives, couples who quarrel and bicker sap their sexual appetites. Some even give up on marital sex and go without it for long periods. They become virtual celibates. Therapist Carl Rogers, author of *Becoming Partners: Marriage and Its Alternatives*, reveals a time of no sexual desire in his own marriage. "During my forties," he wrote, "there

---

The Pleasure Bond, p. 107.

was a period of nearly a year when I felt no sexual desire—for anyone. No medical cause was found." He says his wife's continuing love was the best therapy. "I gradually became sexually normal once again."[*]

Some wives, however, refuse to accommodate their sexual needs to a husband's long period of celibacy. Even a long-faithful wife in her fifties may lash out and break the fidelity bond. In a last-ditch effort before menopause supposedly ends one phase of her sexual identity, she may try adultery to reassure herself that she is still capable of sexual pleasure.

The lines:

> "Hogamous, higamous, men are polygamous
> Higamous, hogamous, women monogamous."[†]

seem no longer to apply. Helen's attitude about her early bandaid affairs appears to substantiate an article in *Psychology Today*[‡] in which Judith Hennessee says that women are not naturally less promiscuous than men. Hennessee says that this kind of thinking reflects a 1950s mentality.

Husbands and wives often lose interest in marital sex because they have other priorities on their mind. Sex becomes another obligation to be met at the end of the day.

"I wanted that master's degree," a 36-year-old nurse said, "and that meant focusing all my energies on it. There were papers to write, reports, reading assignments, exams—no wonder my interest in sex dwindled. I had to put the master's first to the exclusion of everything else. By the time I came home from studying at the library, I could barely crawl into bed next to my sleeping husband."

Other couples lose interest in marital sex because they can't seem to renegotiate their unsynchronized sex lives. Eleanor, a 39-year-old boutique owner, said, "My husband and I had different biological drives. When we got married twelve years ago, he couldn't get

---

[*] Quoted by Flora Davis in *Ladies Home Journal*, September 1980, p. 88.
[†] Quoted by Lois Gould in *Such Good Friends*. Original citation *Eight Lines and Under: An Anthology of Short, Short Poems*, edited by William Cole, Macmillan Co., N.Y., 1967, p. 50, anon.
[‡] "What Do Men Really Want?" by Judith Adler Hennessee, February 1978, p. 113.

enough, and I was the reluctant partner. But now it's the reverse. I have a sexual capacity greater than his. He comes home exhausted, hassled over some customer who's still on his mind. Me? I come home exhilarated, charged up, feeling . . . well, sexy. I remember standing in front of a mirror and looking myself over. I wondered if there was anything wrong with me. I looked good and I felt good. But either he was too tired or too angry. And here I was raring to go. So I figured why waste this gorgeous body on him. Some lucky guy out there was bound to appreciate it. And a 26-year-old boy was the lucky winner."

This wife's attitude is a far cry from the 1950s attitude of Mira, the heroine of Marilyn French's novel *The Woman's Room.* "They had little sex life. Norm was away, or he was tired. But the pattern that had begun at their marriage had enforced itself as unbreakable. Coitus was quick and unsatisfying. Mira lay back and permitted it."*

Few women in the 1980s are likely to lie back and permit it. Even if they did in the first years of their marriage, they are more likely at midlife to expect satisfaction. According to an article in *Harper's Bazaar,*† many women don't discover the joys of sex until 40. "Waists may expand and laugh lines deepen, but as Masters and Johnson observe, 'It appears that women in the middle years . . . are more responsive and more orgasmic than younger women. . . .'" Dr. Judith Bardwick, University of Michigan professor, says: "No doubt about it, older women have the erotic edge. Gray hair, flab, sedentary habits, lack of interest in sex? This is nonsense."‡

At mid-life, a woman may try out a brief "vacation adultery" and find it wonderful. But later on, she changes. She wants a "love of my life," as Helen called Frank. Once sex was physical relief. Now she wants to fuse it with a loving relationship. Donna reported the same reaction in her affair with Adolfo. What she longed for was a relationship, not just sex.

And sometimes an affair has nothing to do with sex. Although the wife's explanation is that she needed more sex, or better sex, or more varied sex—sex may be the only way she can be physically

---

* Page 66.
† "Better Sex Begins at 40," by Abigail McCarthy, October 1980, p. 194.
‡ Page 118.

close to another person. A closeness that has eroded over the years of marriage as other priorities pushed closeness aside.

Yet, most wives don't take a lover. Although their needs have changed too, they seem able to navigate these eddies successfully with the marriage intact. Frequently, they give credit to their husbands. These women say they couldn't have gone back to college or moved into a new career without a husband's support. If he is able to meet her changing needs, somehow, they get through the stormy period, together.

Other women who renegotiate their marriages, who can't restructure their lifestyles, reshuffle their priorities. They say that *semper fidelis* may be a splendid motto for the United States Marines, but for them *always faithful* is no longer a credo essential to their self-image as women.

10

Everyone's Doing It

"I WAS ABSOLUTELY faithful to my wife for ten years. Never thought about another woman. Never looked at other women that way. Until the publishing party at Victor's house. Victor always provided the most interesting people, and he loved to surround himself with great-looking women. But I never considered fooling around.

"But that night Cheryl and I had quarreled, and she said some pretty lousy things to me, which hurt. I found myself dancing with JeriAnne. She wore a white jumpsuit, she had red frizzy hair that brushed my cheek as we danced. We talked about a novel she was working on, and I agreed to look at it. 'You're a very generous guy,' she said, and it made me feel good that she saw it, because only hours before Cheryl had called me selfish.

"Later, when we were leaving, Victor said, 'You really turned on JeriAnne. She'd love to see you again.' He enjoyed his reputation for arranging trysts. 'You want to see her?' I said 'No.' 'Come on,' he said. 'Why miss out?'

"A week went by, and I called Victor for her number."

Like men, a woman can be initiated into an affair at the prompting of a friend who assures her that "Everyone's doing it." When she learns that several women whom she thought were faithful have been enjoying affairs, her first reaction may be astonishment. But on later consideration she may wonder how pervasive affairs are in the lives of her married friends. If the women who are unfaithful are also responsible married women with ties to the community, if they appear to carry on a perfectly "normal" life, if they are also good wives and mothers, she may begin to mull over in her mind questions like these:

"How long have they gotten away with it?"

Which then leads to: "How *do* you get away with it?"

Which leads to: "Could *I* get away with it?"

If the astonishment is not only at the act but also at the perpetrator, an ordinary woman who seems to lack a certain wildness or glamour, the wife may pose other more probing questions:

"I'm better looking, I'm smarter, why can't I enjoy an affair?"

"What am I missing?"

"Is everybody doing it?"

She may think of the men who have approached her and regret turning down an especially attractive man who aroused her. If she has a particularly romantic nature, like Ellen, who danced to records all by herself; if she is bored, like Carol; if she needs stimulation, like Gina—she may be ripe to translate her romantic longings into realities. Prompted by the knowledge that a less "capable" woman is having more fun than she is, she may ask the most important question, "Why not me?"

Is everyone doing it?

A part-time nursery school teacher tells how she was initiated. "A friend of mine confided that she had a lover. She described where they met and what they did. 'He keeps me young,' she said. 'He shapes me up, gives me energy. It's so much fun.' When I made the case for monogamy, she just laughed at me. 'Monogamy is hopelessly archaic. Stash it away in the Smithsonian. The chic way to go in the eighties is to have an affair.' Then she named two other women who cover for each other. I was aghast. I thought about it all afternoon. I went through the motions of serving dinner but what was really on my mind was Sally, and Terri, and Dawn. How could they?"

A contemporary woman receives many messages, often from her closest friends: Sexual exclusivity is dead. Fidelity is obsolete. Modern marriage demands more sensible solutions.

This was the case with Carol, whose first unhappy affair was encouraged by a woman cousin who also happened to be her closest and dearest friend. Carol's cousin, an unhappily married woman, was "making noises about looking for a man." She urged Carol to follow her lead. Up to that point Carol's dissatisfactions with her marriage were dealt with through activity—an endless stream of activity. Four children, a home, music, art, books, and a teaching career all kept her busy and distracted. But when her cousin said "Look, he has a friend," Carol made the decision to have an affair.

Many wives are vulnerable and do *not* make that choice. The taboos against infidelity are too strong for them to overcome. Carol explains the combination of factors that led up to this first short-lived affair. But it was the presence of her cousin as an ally and a mentor which was the catalyst.

Carol's experience isn't unique; a supportive ally is a necessary ingredient for some wives to take the plunge. It may start when a friend confides the details of her own affair, then assures her that it is a wonderful, exciting *extra* in her life. The tempted wife may move slowly.* She may begin by asking questions of her "sophisticated" friend. She wants reassurance. She needs to be urged to take action. When she finally does make the move, she might tell herself it was her friend who pushed her over the brink. Someone else made her do it. The edge of guilt is softened if she can shift the blame.

As we have seen, even wives emotionally committed to long-term marriage may have an affair. Gina insists that her ten-year love affair with Edward is an extra—"a little icing on the cake." That it is her marriage that really counts. She sees herself as a firm believer in marriage, a person committed to her family.

Like other wives who have both a husband and a lover for many years, Gina doesn't want to end the marriage. Some wives continue to have affairs and, Hollywood style, maintain friendships with their former lovers when the affair ends. Lovers may come and go, but the marriage commitment holds fast. This is often called the "civilized" approach. "Even if the sex part ended," Gina says, "I'd still want to be Edward's friend."

---

* Gina waited six months.

Having It Both Ways

A recent *New York* magazine article, by Christina Paolozzi Bellin,* tells a seductively simple story about how high society lives, Here's the formula: a husband, a "successful" one, of course; and "a fantastic lover."

The *in* people, the smart set, the *au courant* know how to live. Keep your husband for status, security, children. But add a lover on the side to do unspeakably erotic things. A lover to turn you young again. To take you dancing all night, like Mrs. Bellin. To transform you, delight you, adore you. Isn't this every woman's dream?

Hold it, you say, that's a large order. At 36 or 41 or 45, your complexion has moved into the dry zone on the Estee Lauder computer. Your fashionably tinted aviator glasses have gone bifocal. And your Scarlett O'Hara waistline has simply . . . gone. Lovers are not breaking down your door. Feeling depressed? So was Mrs. Bellin. "I felt paralyzed," she wrote, "I couldn't move my 36-year-old body." A surgical face lift helped, but what really rescued her was an eighteen-year-old Israeli boy who was "exquisitely handsome, sexy, with a beautiful voice. . . . The boy's visit turned out to be the most exciting six months of my life. Now I can dance for eight hours straight . . . I have all this, thanks to an eighteen-year-old boy named Eyal."

Of such articles are dreams made. *Forum*, a magazine that gives itself the subtitle "The International Journal of Human Relations," served up a double header with two such provocative articles in a single issue:† "Are You Ready to Open Up Your Marriage?" and "Carefree Sex with Strangers."

What does it all add up to?

The promise that any married woman can dive in, too. That having a husband and a lover is not the exclusive domain of the Jet Set. Having it both ways is the wave of the future. You want proof? In the 1950s, the Kinsey statistic testified that one in four wives was unfaithful. In the seventies, *Redbook*'s survey claimed that the ratio was almost one in three. Projections to the year 2000 seem to suggest that anyone who clings to monogamy will be "swimming

---

* "Rock Keeps You Young," June 16, 1978.
† January 1978.

upstream." What the media sells, then, is the message that any wife who wants one can have a lover.

Certainly, the stigma of a love affair has lost its shock value. The climate of opinion has changed. Rock stars who are drug addicts continue to sell records. Movie stars who refuse to marry the father of their baby continue to win awards. Formerly they would have been ostracized. These and other lifestyles are no longer considered deviant. When the ten o'clock news reports murders, muggings, incest, rape, arson, and child molesting, what is so outrageous about a perfectly nice middle-class wife having a discreet affair? It pales in the light of "hard" news.

However, today's permissiveness about extramarital sex is not necessarily a genuinely felt conviction. One woman told me: "Extramarital sex is wonderful. It's perfectly okay." Then she scowled. "As long as it doesn't hit *my* home."

Morton Hunt, author of *Sexual Behavior in the 1970s*, says: "How is one to reconcile the public's current interest in the subject of extramarital sex with its continuing disapproval of it? The glib answer is to say that Americans are hypocritical about sex. . . . A more thoughtful answer might be that the majority of people have always experienced extramarital desires . . . and kept them hidden; in today's climate of open discussion . . . most people continue to disapprove of such behavior because they believe that when it becomes a reality rather than a fantasy, it undermines and endangers the most important human relationship in their lives."*

Once the subject of sex was hidden in fat medical reference books and reserved for professional discussions on biology and human reproduction. Now lesbianism, gay liberation, *ménage à trois*, fellatio, cunnilingus, sado-masochism, and transsexual operations are subjects of book club selections, TV sit-coms, Oscar-winning movies, and Broadway hits. This suggests they are commonplace and that everyone is doing it.

But what is shocking is that alone among this profusion of reportage the fact that married women have lovers is barely touched on. The public image persists: The marriage bond is inviolate and

* Page 256.

sacrosanct to wives, despite the rising statistic that one out of three wives has affairs.

The human potential movement has changed attitudes enormously. In an age of "self actualization" we are instructed to run faster, earn more, be a better lover. Adult classes give courses to shape up mentally, physically, and sexually. *Psychology Today* offers its readers cassettes entitled "Overcoming Shyness," "Getting Rid of Your Fears," and "Mind Expansion Without Drugs." The bestsellers promise infinite self-improvement. You can be your own best friend, make a million in the stock market, even flatten your tummy. All part of the frenetic search for more.

Almost everyone demands to be heard on every human level. Many Americans have gone from compliant to assertive, from apologetic to demanding, from entreating to entitled. They demand job equality, racial equality, sexual equality. They expect fair treatment on issues of overtime pay, welfare, restitution, reparation, compensation, and unemployment. They riot, shout, burn, set off bombs. And these attitudes have altered our sex lives; the demand is for more sex and better sex. *

The restrictions on pleasure are no longer rigidly enforced, nor is it reserved for the young alone. Pleasures of the flesh are permitted. Many women feel less guilt about spending money on creams, depilatories, hair dyes, tanning lotions, diet pills, setting jels, powders, and cosmetics for one purpose: to look younger and more attractive. Today's grandmas don't retreat to ladies' sewing circles. They're out on the tennis court, or preparing to run a marathon, a charity ball, or a law firm. In their forties and fifties and sixties, they are elegantly turned out, as stylish and attractive as their daughters, active women pursuing new goals and allowing themselves sexual pleasure. Even children's sexuality is on display. Commercials for status jeans for children use explicit sexual references.

The women's liberation movement has probably had the most tremendous impact on how women view themselves. The waves of feminism reach deeply into the lives of men and women and

---

* Maxine Schall's book *Limits: A Search for New Values* suggests that the underlying ailment of our time is the quest for unconditional love.

have, to a certain extent, reshaped their relationships. But with a divorce rate that has doubled in a decade,* there is also widespread anxiety. Today's term "splitting" takes the sting out of words like separated and divorced, but cannot lessen the emotional upheaval and deeply felt pain of ending a relationship. Many of us yearn to find "better," more "satisfying" ways to live together: The *Zeitgeist* has changed.

As organized religions lose their power to dictate moral behavior, unmarried couples live together openly and invite their parents for dinner, place both their names on the mailbox, buy houses together, open bank accounts together and travel together. Single women choose to have children without marrying. Divorced fathers fight custody battles to raise their children without a mother. And women marry men younger than themselves, poorer than themselves, shorter than themselves—all no-no's of the past. Even older people raised in stricter moral times make adjustments when their wallets hurt. They live together without marriage for the Social Security advantages of being classified widow or widower. And often their married children and grandchildren applaud them for it.

The effect of this changing climate on our sexual options has been enormous. Today we recognize a range of options once excluded from normal boundaries. The expanding field of sex research has contributed to this. It has earned respectability at many American universities and added weight to our interest in increasing our sexual options. Journalist Jane Brody notes how heavily the field of sex research has been underwritten by government grants. During the Carter Administration *The New York Times* could report "No research application is turned down because it's 'too hot,' although there is a list of no-no areas, including any project that uses surrogate sex partners or involves the researcher or therapist in sexual activity with his subjects or patients."†

As the taboos vanish, the range of normality widens. Sodomy, fellatio, and cunnilingus, once crimes, are now practices openly

---

* According to a *New York Times* article by Anna Quindlen, November 28, 1977.
† January 8, 1978.

acknowledged in many circles. Sex researchers and sex manuals offer explicit instructions on enhancing pleasure.

What about sexual fantasies? Once labeled red flags to diagnose deviant sexuality, they, too, may be considered normal. The fantasies in Nancy Friday's book *Men in Love* include sex with animals, sex with excreta, sex in threesomes and foursomes and groups, peeping and flashing and getting your wife to flash, homoeroticism, incest, sadism, masochism.

Is it only talk, wives wonder? Or is everybody doing it? Classified ads appear for swingers, switchers, and swappers in search of new thrills. Wives talk to other wives, other couples, traditional couples, faithful couples. And many admit that they, too, are wondering if they aren't completely out of step with the times. They note that mechanical aids can be bought over the counter. Norelco's vibrator called Feelin' Good is aimed "to the sensual market,"* according to Carola Crowley, a product manager for the company. A woman can go to a department store and say "charge it." The once taboo act of "jerking off" is public and respectable. When Kinsey revealed that masturbation was widespread, he lifted the curtain on an act which many people believed caused blindness or insanity. In 1966 when Masters and Johnson published *Human Sexual Response* clitoral stimulation became acceptable for women. So vibrator sex became another option.

In a society of many divorced, separated, and widowed women, the woman living alone now had her own fun toy. Some therapists use it to teach non-orgasmic women to achieve orgasm. Shere Hite, author of *The Hite Report,* urged women to employ masturbation. And Lonnie Garfield Barbach's *For Yourself: The Fulfillment of Female Sexuality,* "a top-flight book,"† was written as a guide to achieving orgasm.

In a climate of limitless sexual options, it is easy to be aroused. Barraged by all these forces and their expanded options, many wives are bound to wonder if they are missing out. If their marriage imposes taboos and limitations on their sexual pleasure, they may

* *Esquire*, July 1980, page 56.
† According to Mary Calderone, M.D., Executive Director of the Sex Information and Education Council of the United States.

be afraid to try out some of the new options with their husbands. Do "nice" wives do those things? And if a husband won't, will a lover? As long as the options she chooses are private consensual acts, says the emancipated view, they must not be termed illegal.

Still, many wives are confused. Contemporary women are often told to learn to make attachments and cast them off. A full page ad in *The New York Times*° for example, featured a photograph of a sexy-bra-less woman with her shirt open to the waist, asking: "How do you know when it's time to say goodbye . . . to leave someone you've adored?" The answer was supplied in two parts. One: "If you're married, I think you stay until life is intolerable . . . wouldn't you agree?" Two: "If you're single, you leave when you're not in love with each other anymore or the other person is giving you the fits (behaving badly)." Love, then, by its very nature is transient. Many married women who have lovers see their affair not in moral but in pragmatic terms. Are women becoming more like men? Able to enjoy a fling with little guilt?

Gay Talese, author of *Thy Neighbor's Wife*, wrote about his own affairs: "Like a majority of men, Talese was emotionally committed to a long-term marriage that he wanted to continue. While he had had affairs, he had never wanted to leave his wife for these women, although he continued to admire them and maintain close friendships with many of them."

One cannot deny Talese's observation that the majority of men succeed in having affairs and maintaining a wife, too. Still, Talese finds the times increasingly permissive for women. "While I can't prove it, I think that middle-class American husbands now, more than ever before in American history, can live with the knowledge that . . . their wives have had, or are having, an extramarital affair. I'm not saying that husbands are not bothered by this . . . [but] the contemporary husband, unlike his father and grandfather before him, is not shocked or shattered by such news, is more likely to accept women as sexual beings, and only in extreme cases will he retaliate with violence against his unfaithful wife or male rival. . . ."†

Would women, both feminists and non-feminists, agree? On the

° October 16, 1980, p. D24.
† Page 523.

book jacket for Maria Roy's *Battered Women,* Gloria Steinem says: "We are just beginning to realize that the most dangerous place for women is not in the streets, but their own homes. And those who beat, injure and even murder women are less likely to be muggers or strangers than they are the women's own husbands or lovers." A wife may forgive her husband's affair, but a husband who catches his wife having an affair sometimes feels he has the right to beat her up. The taboos have weakened, but the double standard still applies to extramarital sex. A wife who finds out about her husband's lover is instructed to react with patience, understanding and forgiveness. But the husband who catches his errant wife and then smacks her around is "only giving her what she deserves."

A woman enjoying a brief romp of a few weeks or months can usually avoid detection by her husband, but a long-term love affair spanning many years is much more likely to be discovered. To reduce the risk a woman must take extra precautions: This means lining up excuses, having alibis ready, and preparing contingency arrangements if plans are suddenly changed.

It also means establishing a network of friends who can cover for her during the time she's with her lover.

If a wife's married friends have lovers, they can then provide her with alibis for almost daily trysts. They know the ropes and advise each other about how to avoid pitfalls, how not to get caught, and how to keep a husband at bay. They pretend they are with each other. In the next chapter, you will meet Irena and her friend Marilyn who were each other's cover "on 100 occasions." And, most important, for the women who make up these networks, it may seem as though everybody's doing it.

Despite the feeling that everyone's doing it, some wives with friends having affairs still put off taking a lover of their own. Perhaps Ellen resisted that step because once she took it she would be forced to admit her marriage was in trouble. As long as she went on being faithful, she could delude herself that her marriage was no different from anyone else's. Ellen detected problems and complained that her husband never engaged her whole being, that he didn't arouse her. But she was willing to go on that way because she felt no worse off than her friends: "I didn't see any great excitement among the couples we knew."

For some long-faithful wives an affair is the official declaration that something is seriously wrong with the marriage. Even an imperfect marriage often seems better than the prospect of divorce.

A majority of wives *do* remain faithful—even if some have regrets. As they get older, each lover denied may add a sense of poignancy over an affair missed. But they still opt for monogamy. Perhaps they tell it with a sigh: that in an age of sexual options, they stuck by fidelity.

Other wives remain faithful with a sense of pride. They elect to say, "No, it's not for me." No, to a clandestine one-night stand. No, to a sophisticated, civilized romance. No, to a genuine deeply felt love affair.

To suggest that a book, a movie, or a friend enjoying an affair can by itself induce a faithful wife to change her mind is to deny that there were some powerful motivations at work all along. "Everyone's doing it" is rarely the most compelling of motivations. Hostility, boredom, communication, ego, crises, changing needs, and sex are steel prods in the back. Nevertheless, "Everyone's doing it" is the ubiquitous background music of our time. It sets a catchy rhythm, and whether or not she is really fond of the music, a married woman may find her foot tapping in time to the beat.

11

Adventure: Irena

THE SAYING GOES: At the root of every affair is a problem at home.

However, a small number of women reply, "Problem? No problem. I did it for fun!" These women see an extramarital affair as an adventure. It's a roller coaster ride, a trip to the zoo, a day at the beach, a circus, a thrill. These are women to whom an affair is pure recreation. Their attitude is different from the wives we've discussed. Their marriage is not intolerable. Their husband is not boring or abusive. And their family life is not unsatisfactory. They simply want more adventure than monogamy can provide. They care for their husbands, and they value their marriage. But they also want to be free to enjoy the adventure of outside attachments. They are committed to their marriage but enjoy affairs as "extras." And they say they can handle it.

Not so, according to journalist Natalie Gittelson,* who agrees that more and more women are having affairs, but who issues an age-old warning to wives that the survival of their marriage may be at stake. Men, she feels are better able to handle affairs. Dr. Graham B. Spanier, associate professor at the College of Human Development, Pennsylvania State University, who studied extramarital relations reasons that women respond "more emotionally

* *McCall's*, June, 1980, page 20.

and more intensely to having affairs than men do." And this is why women's affairs are more likely to break up a marriage.

Even if a woman can manage to balance a husband and a lover, she may carry a heavy weight of guilt. However, Gittelson observes that a woman's guilt "appears to decline in direct proportion to her level of fulfillment and satisfaction with 'outside sex.'" In other words, the more satisfying the affair turns out to be, the less guilty a wife feels about it. If that is true, the solution to a guiltless affair may be to find a fantastic lover and enjoy a marvelous adventure.

In *The Liberated Couple*, Susan Cohen says: "We are all indoctrinated with the idea that any other lifestyle besides monogamous, heterosexual marriage is sinful, immoral, or sick."* But some women have gotten over that. They discover that they feel guiltless over extramarital sex.

❂   ❂   ❂

Irena, whom I met at a party and later interviewed in her apartment, was such a woman. What you will hear in Irena's interview may shock or offend. It is not the language of ladies or nice girls, but rather, the language of men. The sensibility that Irena expresses about sex is readily acceptable when subscribed to by a man. Few women feel free to openly acknowledge such feelings. Irena had one long-standing affair and a few "side attractions," and felt no moral qualms. "I never felt guilty about sleeping with another man," she said. Gordon, her long-time lover, is a black man; she is white. She heard about this book and came over to the piano to chat.

She was a darkly pretty woman with huge Sophia Loren almond eyes, vivacious, stylish, with a big toothy smile. There was something theatrical about her, exotic and bohemian, perhaps due to her extravagant gestures and her fluttering purple-nailed hands, or the salty language that punctuated her fast, intense speech. I was surprised to learn that she was 39. She could have been 29. "I've got two kids, 11 and 9. I'm separated," she told me. "Just moved into my own pad with another woman who left her husband and four kids, too. Want to interview me?"

We set up an early evening meeting—6:30 at her place. Her

* Page 172.

apartment mate, Marilyn, would be out visiting her children, who lived with her husband. Irena was a hospital administrator for a Connecticut medical center. "I'll grab a bite on the way home and we'll talk." She scribbled the directions on a napkin, drew me a map, then waved left and right through the exit signs and red lights on the napkin. "Got it?" She folded the napkin into my bag. "You won't be sorry you made the trip. I promise you an interesting story."

When I rang the bell of her townhouse apartment, a cluster of weathered redwood attached homes amidst a leafy wooded setting, there was no answer. I rang, and rang again. Still no answer. I returned to my car and waited fifteen minutes, thirty minutes, worrying all the time that her party bravado had given way to doubts. Through the trees, I kept my eyes on her doorway.

She arrived on the run, trotting toward her townhouse, fumbled with her key and let herself in. I waited five minutes to give her time to unwind, then I rang the bell.

She greets me buttoning a madras shirt over her jeans, with her feet bare. She is breathless, rumpled, and harried. A frozen pizza is shoved into a counter top oven–broiler, and a punctured can of coke stands beside it.

"They kept me late, so I didn't have time to eat. Wanna piece of pizza? Something to drink?"

"Tea?" I ask.

She finds a teabag and puts the water on—all the time talking. This woman is verbal, dramatic, fiery, and opinionated. We sit around a dinette table in a small alcove attached to the tiny kitchen. The apartment is strewn with unpacked boxes and cartons. "We're still moving in, we've barely unpacked. See?" She waves an arm toward the living room and two bedrooms beyond it, and bites into a hot slice of pizza.

"I was married at 22. No virgin. I'd had lovers, many of them. Though I never had an orgasm. When I married Henry, I felt very warm and tender toward him. I loved him, I felt a warmth and tenderness and love. No great sexual excitement, but it didn't

199

matter because there were other qualities that we shared that were more important.

"I met Gordon before my first anniversary, and we've been lovers, off and on, for 16 years. Oh, I've had other men along the way, too. But Gordon—well he's something special.

"Maybe I was scripted by my mother. She had a lover, too. I called him Uncle Abe. My mother was an immigrant who left Poland when she was 16. She didn't speak a word of English and she went to live with her sister, became a housemaid to her sister's six kids. She married my father to escape from her sister's house and she didn't have me until she was 40. My father also had a hard, tough life. In and out of orphanages. Both of them uneducated. But my mother—hey, she was a gutsy, very bright woman. Incisive wit. Biting. Very strong. And domineering. Would have been a dynamite lady if she had had opportunities. Anything I have in terms of vitality, intelligence, brassiness I get from her. She was one helluva broad!

"My father? He was just a nice, quiet man. Stupid, bovine. They fought like cats and dogs. He gambled, owed I.O.U.s, and she didn't respect him. I think he was impotent. She had this lover, Abe, who also came from Poland. And she told me Abe was my real father. It's a very early memory, but I see it all in my mind's eye. She was sitting at the kitchen table with her friend, Iris, and she called me into the room.

" 'Irena,' she said, she was laughing. 'Tell Iris who your real father is. Go on, tell her.' I looked at her because it was a secret we shared and she told me never to tell anyone. 'No, it's all right, you can tell Iris.'

"So I said, 'Abe. Abe is my father.' "

She has eaten the whole pizza and washed it down with coke. "Lousy pizza." Then she looks at me hard.

"I have had years of therapy—years!—trying to decide whose daughter I am—years of misery over it. At this point, it doesn't make one fucking difference. I couldn't stand Abe, and I couldn't respect my father, so maybe I've always been looking for a father figure—who knows? Anyhow, when I was 14, I saw a picture of

Abe and his daughter at a family gathering in our house, and I saw that Abe's daughter and I looked alike. We looked like sisters. Who knows?"

She shrugs to assure me it's of no interest to her anymore.

"I wouldn't say I was a battered child, but my mother hit me regularly. She had this thing about my eating and she'd hit me if I didn't eat. I had a narrow esophagus. She sent me to the hospital to have it stretched, and the doctor told her that if she made sure I ate, it would stretch. So she thought she was doing me a favor by forcing me to eat. She'd beat the daylights out of me if I didn't. It screwed up my head for a lot of years. All kinds of oral problems: thumb sucking, smoking, incessant chattering. I hated her viciously, hated her for years. Hated her, and feared her, and loved her. She died a year after I got married.

"When I met Henry he was a psychological wreck, an anxiety neurotic, unable to function. He didn't work; he was in school, but he subsequently dropped out because he was overcome with anxiety.

"So why did I take on a guy like this for a husband?"

She pushes her chair back and crushes the pizza box which was her plate into the garbage can along with the empty coke can.

"He needed me. He loved me. I made him feel better. I soothed his fevered brow. I supported him. I gave him strength. I was Florence Nightingale.

"Also, he was very bright and cultured with a capital C. Compared to my impoverished, lower-class background, that looked good to me. You want to know what my mother told me? The best thing that could happen to me would be to become a secretary— that's as high as she could aim for me. And she didn't approve of Henry. She had no tolerance for psychological problems. To her he was a malingerer, a lazy bum. He was calling me up in the middle of the night to come running to take care of him. I loved it. He was my baby. It made me feel good.

"Still, I took a lover before our first anniversary. And for 16 years

I always had a lover—Gordon plus a few others. And he never knew, never saw it. Not 'til the end.

"I need freedom. Excitement and stimulation. Not Henry. He couldn't stand to be separated from me, to know he couldn't reach me, touch me. When I made Phi Beta Kappa in college, I went off for a weekend in Cambridge and he put up such a fuss. He would have put a goddamn leash around my neck, but I went anyhow. Once he smacked me because I came home late after having a cup of coffee with a guy in class. But he never hit me again until the night Marilyn broke up with her husband and her husband beat her up. Henry worked himself into such a frenzy, he beat me up, too. Outside of those two incidents, he never laid a hand on me. He knew it blows my mind—any kind of physical violence—maybe because my mother knocked me around.

"We didn't have children for six years. He didn't want kids in the beginning, and neither did I because I was terrified of the influence of my mother, afraid I'd be the same kind, that I wouldn't be a fit mother. By that time Henry was working and functioning well. He was a teacher, a very good teacher, a fine teacher because he related very well to children. He also became a good father, absolutely adored our daughter, a bit jealous of our son.

"Why did I leave Henry after all those years? I was thinking about it the other day. How I do things strangely. I'll think about something for years and do nothing about it. Then one day I decide *that's it!* That's how I quit smoking. That's how I learned to drive a car. That's how I left my husband. I spotted this ad in the paper. I knew I had someplace to go. So I left Henry and the kids, and Marilyn left her husband and four kids, and we decided to live together.

"I have to tell you about Marilyn. She's been my closest friend for 19 years. We're living together, but we're not sleeping together. We've considered it, but we're afraid it would break up the friendship. Marilyn and I have shared so much over the years. We made love in the same room—with her husband and mine. Once with different lovers. We covered for each other, lied for each other, schemed for each other. We have been each other's cover stories on 100 occasions. So why mess it up now? We talk about our fantasies: a threesome—us and a guy—a little orgy. We haven't ruled out a lesbian relationship between us. It might occur at some point in the future, but right now we don't want to endanger a lifelong relationship. So we're keeping it platonic.

"Let me tell you about Gordon, my long-standing lover. Gordon is black. I met him in the '60s, and in those days we felt very proud of our integrated relationship. It was finals week when I started sleeping with him. A pretty story. We met in the library to study together and we got hungry so we went to his place. I was a bride, married less than a year. We were sitting on the couch reading and talking and getting snuggly, and things started to get warm. And I thought what the hell, what are we fighting this for? So we made love. That was the beginning. We're still lovers, though I've had men in between and he got married and divorced. I don't have strong sex drives. Once, twice a week is enough. I don't get real horny. It's just something I like. But when I like it, I want it. If I'm attracted to a man, I go after him. And I don't rest until I'm in bed with him."

The thrill of conquest which Irena describes has often been articulated by men when they talk about their affairs. Rarely by women.

"If I lose interest, or someone else comes along who captures my interest, why not? Anyhow, Gordon is quite bright, quite highly trained, very well paid—a doctor. He's over 6 feet—I like tall men—and was skinny as a rail when we became lovers. Later when he got married, the marriage made no difference in our relationship. We slept together the day before the wedding, and again the week he came back from his honeymoon. Why should marriage interfere? I like excitement. I like thrills and chills. Even though I'm non-orgasmic in intercourse, I find sex physically satisfying and I love to screw like crazy.

"Maybe I never wanted my husband to be my lover. Maybe it's all mixed up in that Freudian shit about how if he's my lover he can't be my father—which is what I wanted: a father. Anyhow, all those years of therapy never figured it out. So I don't go anymore. I think a lot has to do with control—with being in control and losing control. I've been high on pot in order to lose control. Because I'm a very controlling person. I'm manipulative, pushy, domineering.

Oh, mama has nothing on Irena! I don't appreciate it in myself and probably it's part of my inability to experience orgasm: I can't let go. But I masturbate very nicely. I can have orgasms when I masturbate. I wouldn't let Henry masturbate me because I wasn't going to let him control my orgasms. They were mine. Besides I knew my hands better than his and I could control them. I would even go down on him, but I wouldn't let him go down on me. See, I enjoy giving pleasure, I enjoy being in control.

"But Gordon—ho! Gordon and I did *everything* to each other. We explored with each other, we experimented with each other, we did it all."

She chuckles over a private thought she is enjoying and decides to tell me.

"After Gordon got married, you know what he told me? 'Nobody makes love the way we do.' I'll never forget that. Maybe it was the way our bodies meshed, how we fit together. We were both skinny, light and narrow. He said skinny people make the best lovers. He didn't overwhelm me, he wasn't a massive bulk. I like men built the way I am: narrow and lean and long. I cannot stand fat. His hips fit between my legs and our movements, our bodies, worked together. I could sit across the room from Gordon and feel excited. He didn't have to touch me. We'd walk down the street and find ourselves running, running to get home. It was the most incredible, passionate, passionate affair. I didn't experience orgasm with him either, but it was tremendous excitement. I was never frustrated. I loved to be held. I love to feel a man inside me, to feel him moving, the excitement, the pleasure, it's all very satisfying.

"When I masturbated, I would be thinking about Gordon and I'd get so aroused I'd have an orgasm. With Gordon I had the feeling I was sexually so attractive, I was irresistible. With a husband . . . well, you eventually get the feeling you have to perform—it's a wife's duty. Oh, I continued to have sex with Henry. It was a fuck. I'd just as soon go to bed with him and not have the hassle. I don't think we ever missed a week without getting laid.

"Then four years ago, my husband developed Hodgkins disease.

It's crazy, but this period was the best time we ever had in our marriage. A six-month period when things were super. I was taking care of him again. I was working full-time and we had money and I was feeling good about myself. Really super. I was smoking pot, willing to experiment. And I had Gordon—always there was Gordon—my super lover. Somehow at this time I could see Henry as just another man. Not a husband, not a father—more as a stranger. Strangers I have no problem fucking. Maybe it was the pot."

She laughs, daring me to register disapproval.

"Look. I would never do anything but pot. And lately I don't even like the way I've been reacting. So I smoke very, very little. One joint, enough to get high, not stoned. I did it the way some people come home to a cocktail. To unwind after the day's work. Anyhow, Gordon is not into pot. He's a drinker, he never smokes.

"What sustained my affair with Gordon over all those years? Maybe a lot of the same things that sustained my relationship with my husband. Gordon became dependent on me for solace, for talk, for discussion, for advice. I became, and to this day I remain, his closest friend. When anything significant is happening in his life, I'm the first to know, I'm the one he comes to. We've remained constant friends and lovers over the years. It's a very nurturing situation.

"There was a long period in which I was totally faithful to Gordon. He was my only lover. I was living in the suburbs with two small kids. Who the hell was I going to sleep with? No likely material there. Uh uh. I wouldn't sleep with my friends' husbands. No, there was no opportunity for other men.

"So when Gordon came to see me, I'd sneak a day, an afternoon away. My favorite thing was . . ."

She giggles at what she is about to tell me.

"Mother's Day weekends! I used to tell Henry to give me a weekend in New York for Mother's Day. I'd stay at the Barbizon Plaza and do all the things I told Henry I was going to do. Ballet, theater, museums, shopping on Fifth Avenue. I'd go to Saks and Bendel and

Bergdorf. I would do all that. But I'd do it with Gordon! He was there waiting for me. We'd do it together. Then late Saturday afternoon, I'd run around like crazy doing some frantic shopping so I could bring home things besides *Playbills*.

"On other occasions, I'd manage to get rid of the kids when Gordon came over. Or I'd put the baby to sleep upstairs and we'd make love downstairs. He'd come to the house. There were a few close calls. I remember one time. . . ."

She chuckles.

"Henry was supposed to go away and he came home unexpectedly to change his clothes. I knew Gordon was on his way over, so I stayed down at the end of the driveway pretending to be pruning a rosebush so I could wave him off. Luckily, Henry left before Gordon arrived, but it was close, damn close. I loved it, the excitement, the thrill of it. I loved having a black lover. My lovers were usually black. And it's not because they've got longer dicks. I think it's because for a white woman it's forbidden fruit. Forbidden fruit is frowned on by everyone. So it's more exciting.

"Gordon and I—oh we used to do such crazy things. Go into the subway and drive old ladies crazy. We'd smooch and cuddle, and he'd put his arm around me, and I'd kiss him, and he'd kiss me. Doing something awful was such fun. We used to get a big charge out of sticking our tongues out at society. There was a long streak of childishness in that, sure. But over the years there was also a good deal of tenderness in our relationship, too. A good deal of warmth. I was treated like a princess by black men.

"And Gordon is such a superior lover. He has such freedom of movement. A lack of inhibitions. There's a body rhythm, an electricity about him. Oh, I know it has to do a lot with forbidden fruit. I know I chose somebody that my mother would definitely disapprove of. Also it was forbidden because I was married. To leave your husband and go off with a black lover, that's forbidden, too.

"I'm not going to make generalizations. But for me it's a very simple and easy thing. I say: I want to go to bed with you because an affair is fun, it's pleasure. I don't want to marry you. We're not going to run off together, not going to get involved. But you turn me on, okay? I want to make love to you. It's very open. Very elemental. Very simple. It's a zipless fuck. *I* want to do it, *you* want to do it. The hell! *Let's do it.*

"An affair is absolutely ego blowing. Look, I'm not promiscuous like, 'Hey, baby, let's fuck,' the kind of shit you get in a singles bar. I like being wooed and courted. It's a tremendous turn-on. And there's no guilt involved. I just want to make love because it feels good. It's something Gordon and I both enjoy. A very nice kind of feeling. And when it's over, we say, 'Shit, that was good!'

"Sex is easy to get. But when you find someone that it's special with, that's something you want to hold on to. Maybe eventually lovers turn into husbands, to some extent that's true and the thrill is gone. But even when I saw Gordon regularly, I was constantly turned on by him. Over that whole period of . . . maybe 12 years at least, I was faithful to him. More or less. But the time came when I didn't feel obliged to be faithful. I was seeing him only twice a year. I wanted to do my thing.

"But I'm very selective, see? I still have feelings about one lover at a time. Serial monogamy. I'm still very monogamous in a lot of ways. And I consciously prefer single men. Because I don't want to be 'the other woman' in somebody's life. I don't give a shit about the man. If he'll be unfaithful with me, he'll be unfaithful with somebody else. But I don't want to be the instrument to hurt another woman. I don't want to break up a marriage. All I want to do is make love. Have an affair. Be his lover. Be his friend.

"I can sleep with a guy just for the sheer pleasure of doing it. I don't have to get emotionally involved. I don't get possessive. I don't feel guilty. I don't make *must* and *should* judgments. Fidelity was never *in* with me. I just make demands on myself and the people I'm with, that's all. I never try to hurt anyone. So I really don't have any guilt. I don't think Gordon would have gone through with his wedding if I wasn't there. He had a fever, see? And I worked a few blocks away. He was sick as a dog and I went over to make lunch and feed him and take care of him. So I slept with him, too. We joked about it later.

"Why should his marriage change anything? We were lovers for so many, many years. We'll *always* be lovers. If he appeared in an hour, right now, I'd feel the same way. I would always sleep with Gordon.

"He's not as pretty as he was when we were both young and beautiful. But it's good, still good. He says to me: 'Goddamit, Irena, you still look as good to me as ever, and I'm fat.' And I say: 'So lose your goddamn belly.' But I still love him and I feel tenderly toward him.

"No, I wouldn't want my daughter to have the details of my life because I don't want to script her the way my mother scripted me."

She grows defiant, angry when I ask if her children have been hurt.

"I *never* damaged her the way my mother did. I *never* told her her father wasn't her father. I *never* presented her with my lover and told her to call him Uncle. She loves her father. She's also very strong, very independent, big mouthed, sarcastic, very biting. She and my son remain in the house with my husband because it's better that way. I see them. I bring them here because we want to maintain some stability in their lives. The same schools, the same friends, the same schedule for continuity. I'm at peace with myself about the kids. And now . . . hey! I have a room of my own. See, I never had a room to myself."

She is perky again, flashing her toothy smile.

"Ever. Anywhere. In my whole life. I finally have one! It's *my* space. If I want the kids to sleep over and share my space, it's okay. But I can send them home. Look, they each have a room of their own. A room they can close the door on.

"It's a substantial change in their lifestyle, but they'll make it. Look, if I could make it, anybody could. I do not subscribe to the bullshit that you stay together for the sake of the children. If my mother and father had been divorced, I would have been better off for it. Henry's parents, too; they waited till we got married to get divorced. You're not doing your children any favor by staying in a bad marriage. That's chicken shit.

"After I nursed Henry through two years of cancer and a nine-month bout with radiation, I'd had it. Plus the heart-rending misery of facing the possibility I could be left a widow with two young children. Having a lover during that period kept the marriage going. I would have gone out of my mind without Gordon.

"Look, I always took my fun where I could find it. I had to have that freedom to do my own thing. There was a long time that I loved my husband. He was a good, kind, and honest person, a good provider. Who would leave a man like that?

"It's funny. I saw Gordon just two months ago and he was lamenting the fact that he didn't marry me long ago when we were kids. He loves me now. He's always loved me. And he says he should have married me then. He wants to marry me now, now that we're both free. But I want to keep him as my lover. Living with him would be terrible. I don't want to cook for him. I don't want to get involved with his laundry. No day-to-day basis. I love him as my lover, my friend. That's what I want. All the whipped cream and none of the shit. You get the whipped cream with a lover. It's exciting, adventure, forbidden fruit.

"Every marriage is a unique situation. A hundred years ago if a married couple didn't have passionate feelings for each other, they weren't miserable. Maybe they had lovers on the outside—rare for women, but not uncommon for men. And they stayed married. They were civilized about it. But we're living in an era of romance. You have to love your husband *forever*, feel passionate about him *forever*. That's bullshit! There is absolutely nothing in this life that is eternal. And passion is certainly one of the most fleeting things.

"I got married to Henry for the right reasons. I saw things in my husband that were more important than fleeting sexual attraction, important reasons to marry him. But . . ."

Her eyes widen with a touch of mischief.

". . . I saw other options, too. That's what broke up our marriage. Because Henry found out I was screwing around. Look, if two people marry and they believe in exclusivity, well, hurray for them! Let them practice it. But what happens when romance goes out the window? When the husband develops a pot belly and he doesn't turn you on anymore? You should still enjoy sex. That's why women are out there searching. For passion. On the outside. Wherever they can find it. More and more women are going to cheat. Absolutely. It's the reality. The difficulty. . . ."

She laughs ruefully and shrugs, then throws up her hands.

". . . the difficulty is this. I have never met a man who is willing to share his woman. I don't think women have as much difficulty sharing men. They've been conditioned to think men are natural philanderers, so they're bound to fool around. Your husband cheats on you, but you'd be stupid to kick him out.

"Lenny Bruce said men would fuck mud. A woman has to love a man, but men would fuck mud. Well, I got news for Lenny. I could fuck mud, too. If the mud is good, I can fuck it. I don't think there's anything holy about sex. No. I don't have to be in love with somebody to sleep with him. I certainly have to like the guy, sure. But I don't have to get emotionally involved.

"I think it's possible for a woman to have it both ways. It just depends on whether or not husbands can deal with it. It worked fine for me until my husband found out. After all those years when I conducted myself so brilliantly—all those years with Gordon and a few others . . . and I blew it! When he found out, instead of lying, I confessed. I spilled my guts out. Maybe because he had Hodgkins at the time. I said to myself: Your husband has cancer and you're fucking around. For years I conducted a number of serial affairs, with Gordon as my primary lover without any difficulty. I had no problems with them. I'm very good at organizing. That's my job. Also, I have a lot of energy, always had a lot of energy, always doing more than one thing. You know what generates energy? A lover! I got most of my energy out of my affairs. They were the spark of my vitality. They keep you going. Then . . . I blew it."

She turns quiet suddenly. She pauses.

"At times I feel furious with myself for requiring the reassurance of a man. That's the thing that bothers me. That dependence on a man drives me crazy.

"When Henry found the receipt from the drugstore for my extra diaphragm, I could have lied my way out. I tried at first. Then I promised I'd never do it again. We had a big brawl—a big, big, *big* brawl. But I wouldn't sign a loyalty oath. I wouldn't mind if Henry fooled around—why begrudge me the same pleasure? But he couldn't stand the idea of my sleeping with anybody. *That's what broke up the marriage. He could not deal with the fact that I could sleep with another man. Well, I could!* One man for pleasure and one for practicality. I have no problem with that. But he couldn't stand sharing me. It was a tremendous put-down on him as a man. So I left and took my first apartment. I wanted my freedom.

"I don't think you should call it cheating. The contract people make when they get married, forsaking all others, that's bullshit! The agreement between people should be to try not to hurt each other."

Betty expressed this, too. She said she tried to lead a good life and not hurt anyone. That if there is a God, He won't disapprove because the one thing she never wanted to do was hurt her husband.

"I never took a lover to get back at my husband. I never took a lover to get even with him. I never took a lover to spite him. Or hurt him. So I never felt guilty about sleeping with another man. Exclusivity is unrealistic, it's an untenable situation. Getting involved with exclusivity is what leads to pain. Exclusivity doesn't work. Marriage doesn't work either. Faithfulness doesn't work. Fooling around doesn't work. Separation doesn't work. Divorce doesn't work. Being single doesn't work. Nothing works. Nothing is perfect.

"I'm 39 and we're into the 1980s, so I have options that women in the 1940s and 1950s didn't have. They were raised with 'You don't love your husband? Tough shit! Make the best of it.' And they did.

"Know something? Maybe they have the right idea.

"I would have been happy enough to have continued having lovers all my life while staying married. I would have been delighted to do that. But my husband couldn't accept it."

❖   ❖   ❖

Irena's motivations for her affairs were: excitement, thrills, and fun. She says what many men say: I took my fun where I could find it. One may wonder how Irene could enjoy sex without orgasms. Although she claims to find great pleasure in sex—"I love to screw like crazy"—she did not experience orgasms with her husband or her lover. What was the source of her pleasure?

Irena seems to be a woman who feels safe only when giving pleasure, when she is in control. She cannot let go. During lovemaking, Irena experienced union without explosion. She felt this was satisfying.

In the year 1900, American life expectancy was a great deal shorter. And if one expected life to be shorter, so was the marriage. However, people today expect to live into their seventies and eighties. They have been granted a much longer adult life, at least as a statistical average. In 1900, the bride who married in her twenties could expect to have 25 or 30 years with her husband, and if the marriage proved unsatisfactory she had few options open to her. Today, that picture has changed drastically. To continue to regard monogamy and exclusivity as essential *through 50 or 60 years of adult life* seems a harsh sentence to many women and men. Only in recent times has absolute fidelity within monogamy become a stricture. Perhaps for some women, as for most men, it is not the most natural way. As the French assume, a wife may have a lover, as a husband will have a mistress. A *certain* fidelity—but absolute fidelity?

A school crossing guard told me: "I think monogamy is too much of a pressure to lay on a woman for 50, 60 years of marriage. I have a strong sex drive and I like variety, so I'd be a fool to limit all my sex to one man. I love my husband. But I love me, too. I'm 38. Maybe that's a nervous age for women. I've never felt so alive and electric and bubbling with energy. It's a helluva burden to hang on to that one man–one woman thing your whole lifetime. Not when there's so much fun waiting out there. It's a new world, and you don't have to worry about getting pregnant. You gotta get with it."

Some wives say there's an enormous difference between marital sex and extramarital sex. Lovemaking with a husband is often "goal-oriented"—to accomplish orgasm or release of tension—and some experts warn this is a sure means to defeat passion. But lovemaking with a lover is playful and deliciously experimental.

The participants are there for *fun* and they want to please each other. So their lovemaking involves a lot more than penetration. The sweetest pleasures of the bed are not "accomplishments" like achieving multiple orgasms or experiencing blockbuster orgasms —but fun.

Ellen pointed out the differences. If her husband didn't want sex, she was happy to turn over and go to sleep. But sex with her lover was pure "fun." He would bathe, scrub, and powder her before making love to her. She said, "I never enjoyed anybody so much in my life . . . such a fun person."

It is this adventurous spirit that makes extramarital sex more pleasurable. Lovers take more time to be experimental, to arouse their partner, and to engage in sex play. As one woman put it: "My husband's approach is business as usual. My lover is always looking for new ways to please me."

A great deal depends, of course, on a person's need for variety. Some people are pleased with the predictable sameness a routine provides. Others need adventure, and just as they value gourmet cooking they want gourmet lovemaking in their lives.

Wives who take lovers for the fun of it may not be in the mainstream, but they exist. They appreciate a more erotic repertoire than one partner can provide. And they see no sin in that.

Monogamy implies ownership, and many people oppose this on principle. They believe in "recreational adultery." They expect their affairs to be impermanent and they do not need to invest a strong emotional bond in an outside partner.

Victoria Woodhull, who ran for President in 1872, supported a plank of free love when she ran against Ulysses S. Grant. "I have an inalienable, constitutional, and natural right," she said, "to love whom I may, to love as long or as short a period as I can, to change that love everyday if I please. And with that right neither you nor any law you can frame can interfere." Like Woodhull, some modern women feel constancy is not a virtue. They feel free to love whom they wish, and marriage is not to interfere with that freedom.

An affair can be many things. For adventurous women it's Romance. Magic. Passion. Fun. A lover provides alternatives a husband does not. Spontaneity. Excitement. Novelty. To some the fact that an extramarital affair is forbidden is the spicy ingredient that adds a special flavor. Besides sex, an affair is a high, the first rush of getting it on with a new person.

The *Redbook Report on Female Sexuality* confirms much in Irena's story. One out of five unfaithful wives—in other words 6 percent of *all* wives—is content with her marriage and has an affair simply for adventure. *Redbook* calls this the 6% solution.* These women are ". . . a substantial minority (who) happily enjoy their husbands *and* their lovers."† These women confound researchers. The prevailing opinion is still that adultery is a symptom of problems in the marriage. The happily married wife who enjoys a lover as recreation is still impossible to accept. But these 6 percent do it! Sometimes they are surprised at their own ability to juggle the two relationships. "I can't believe it. Me! I'm having an extramarital affair." Even if they are married to attentive, affectionate men they care about, they want an affair as that "extra." Often they feel married to *two* husbands: their legal husband, and the other, their ideal husband. They all claim an affair is fun. It is a word used over and over again. Carol enjoyed the *fun* of getting dressed up for her lover. Even Betty admitted it was *fun.* "It was fun, a fun kind of fright. An adventure." Carol explains her need for *excitement.* "I needed *more.* More adventure. More excitement. More sex. See, an affair is full of excitement. And fun! The secrecy. The excitement keeps me way up there. All keyed up. High." Aren't these some of the same reasons men have always given for affairs?

Sometimes a woman who married young feels she may have missed something. Perhaps she was a virgin or a girl with very limited sexual experiences. After 10 or 15 years of fidelity and a happy marriage, she gets a crazy, wild desire to try another man. Now, quick, before it's too late and her courage deserts her.

Nancy, a bright 34-year-old graduate student and mother of two, told me, "My fling with Kurt was pure adventure. It meant absolutely nothing other than the fact that I wanted to try out sex sans husband. It was pure indulgence, and I found it exciting. Why

---

* Other estimates of "vacation adultery" range as high as 12% according to *Psychology Today,* May, 1980, page 75.
† Page 142 (*Redbook Report*).

should I lay a guilt trip on myself over that? It didn't take anything away from my husband, and it made me feel devilish. Maybe if I had gotten it out of my system when I was 18 or 20, I wouldn't feel this way. But I do. I had a yen. I felt restless. I had to satisfy it."

An aspiring playwright told me about her fling. "I have to admit I was thinking of having an affair for a long time—even daydreaming about other men. I wanted a new experience, a relationship with a little mystery to it. I had just finished a one-act play, and I was feeling high. I felt adventurous, like breaking out. The fact that I love the guy I'm married to doesn't mean I couldn't feel horny for somebody else. So when Rob came along, I said, 'Why not?' An affair is a wonderful tool for a playwright and a wonderful experience when you're feeling antsy, restless."

Fran describes herself as "a restless type" and says her love affair with Charles "embellishes" her life. "Maybe because he has the same kind of humor I have. He appreciated my jokes. We laughed and laughed and had such a good time."

Many women—like Carol, Ellen, Fran, and Gina—describe their love affairs in glowing terms. Do they exaggerate "to justify the affair"? Or are romance and excitement for these women genuine turn-ons? Do they have *extra* needs for excitement beyond those of other women? Is Irena, for example, only a special case representing a small number of women who crave adventure?

Men have always paid homage to risk. The nattily dressed gambler who played for high stakes was the hero of many a western movie. So was the macho hero who risked his life fighting a war, hunting a wild buffalo or harpooning a great whale. He was called "manly." To be "womanly" was the opposite. Womanliness consisted of standing by, watching and waiting—passively accepting what fell across your path. To avoid risk was an attractive feminine trait. Some of that has changed. But a good deal hangs on. Men may call the woman who risks and plays for high stakes a ballsy bitch.

Irena's behavior may outrage some, yet Irena establishes standards for her behavior. "I still have feelings about one lover at a time," and "I consciously prefer single men . . . I don't want to be the instrument to hurt another woman . . . I never try to hurt anyone."

Irena responds almost exactly as many adulterous men do. "I can sleep with a (partner) just for the sheer pleasure of doing it. I don't have to get emotionally involved." These remarks do not often come from a woman's lips. It is difficult for many to accept that *there are some women who feel exactly as men do about their extramarital affairs: that it's a helluva lot of fun and an exciting adventure.*

The excitement of the forbidden is rarely absent in an affair. Almost every woman I interviewed paid tribute to its value as a turn-on. Women who value adventure realize that what they are doing is dangerous and risky—that if they get caught, the affair could be abruptly cut off. Knowing that the end could come at any time adds a sense of urgency to each encounter. It is high drama and intrigue and, therefore, that much sweeter.

Linda Wolfe, author of *Playing Around*, says, "We tend to view women's adultery as rising out of reaction rather than self-propulsion ... I have come to see that women have many nonretaliatory, urgent personal reasons for their extramarital affairs . . . (women) whose marriages were sound and even successful, who bore no grudges toward their husbands, and who acted out of imperative personal longings for adventure and variety."*

> Marriage is slavery ... Human personality must develop quite freely. Marriage impedes this development; even more than that, it often drives one to "moral crimes," not only because forbidden fruit is sweet, but because the new love, which could be perfectly legitimate, becomes a crime.

So wrote Nelly Ptaschkina in her *Diary* on October 25, 1918. Almost half a century later, Sylvia Plath expressed similar feelings in *The Bell Jar.*

> I never wanted to get married. The last thing I wanted was infinite security, and to be the place an arrow shoots off from. I wanted change and excitement and to shoot off in all directions myself, like the colored arrows from a Fourth of July rocket.†

* Page 242.
† Chapter 7.

It would be easy to say that women who express such feelings shouldn't marry. Certainly, those who know that they won't be able to abide by the exclusivity contract probably shouldn't undertake a conventional marriage. Some women *are* choosing to remain single. They ignore pressures to marry and have children. But others value the long-term intimacy marriage can provide.

Even those who enjoy recreational adultery do not want to terminate the relationship. They do not want to hurt their husbands. They are convinced—as Irena was—that their husbands would not tolerate sharing them with another man. These women are in a bind.

If a woman remains faithful forever and does not experience the adventures she longs for, she could wind up hating her husband and viewing him as her warden and oppressor. But if she has affairs and confesses them, this will wound her husband and perhaps damage the marriage beyond repair, as Irena did. The solution for such women is to have a clandestine, secret affair that is hidden from the world. They believe they can enjoy the adventure of having a husband and a lover, too. Of having it both ways.

12

THE NEW FIDELITY:
THE COMPOSITE WOMAN

AT THE INCEPTION of a marriage, the participants usually think of it as lasting "forever." For many, "forever" arrives in the form of desertion or divorce. Even so, an affair is almost always of shorter duration than a marriage. It is an excursion—a trip, not a voyage—or, as the movie put it, a "brief encounter," however intense.

Marriage, romantic as its origins may be, is a relationship established by law, a contract that is binding on both parties, rarely dissolved without lawyers and a prolonged battle in and around courts that have jurisdiction over the parties, but no special knowledge or skill in the human matters they oversee.

An affair begins as a voluntary relationship, as do most marriages. The difference is that affairs remain voluntary. Two people become a couple in their own eyes and perhaps in the eyes of a few close friends. They see each other, love each other, and stay together because they want to rather than because they have to. They are not bound by children, by religion, by pressures of their community. They are bound by their feelings for each other.

This book has reported not on premarital affairs or affairs between single people who are free to choose a partner, but on affairs that come after marriage, when the woman is legally not free to do as she pleases with a man other than her husband, but who does it anyway. In fact, it is a report about more than one third of all married women, and it has contained some surprises.

Married women who have had an affair, however much they get caught in the crossfire of their conscience and their needs, very rarely regret it when they look back. For many it has been an enriching, involving experience. For some the riches gained simply consist of the knowledge that an affair is not their way of life.

Drawing on the women whose stories you've read, plus the more than one hundred other interviews conducted over three years, the following picture emerges of the kind of woman who has an affair. Although the circumstances of their lives varied widely, and their backgrounds and personalities were very different, these women share certain characteristics. Not every woman has every one of these qualities, but a composite is a useful way of examining a widespread phenomenon.

Guilt Free
1. The wife who is having it both ways is a relatively guilt-free person. She is not religious, and she doesn't think in terms of sin or evil, heaven and hell. She doesn't regard herself as a fallen woman.

High Energy
2. The wife who takes a lover has a high energy level. She is well organized and knows how to juggle the competing demands of her time and energy. She doesn't fall apart easily or panic under pressure.

Attractive
3. She is a fairly attractive woman. Although she may not be beautiful, she is a woman who cares about her looks, is aware of fashion, and takes pride in her appearance.

Working
4. She is probably a working woman, out in the world and meeting people every day. She is not locked away in a child-centered house where opportunities for dalliance are limited to the Fuller Brush Man.

Young
5. She may be of any age—twenty or sixty—her years are no

barrier. But the most active period for taking a lover seems to be during her thirties or forties. Women who have affairs don't generally begin after fifty. They start earlier, then often continue into the mature years.

Middle Class

6. The wife who has a love affair is not necessarily pampered, rich, a jet setter, or a princess. Nor is she so poor she's fighting to put bread on the table. She is very often a middle-class woman.

Not Abnormal

7. Although she may have sought the help of a marriage counselor or a therapist, she is not any more neurotic than most of us.

Raised Consciousness

8. Her consciousness has been raised, often by the women's movement or by a life experience. She has a high level of expectation, so she demands much of herself.

Takes Charge

9. She likes to take charge of her life, and does not assume a passive role. When faced with frustration she will find a way out. She chooses a lover after she has failed to communicate with her husband or he has failed to respond.

Right Timing

10. Timing and opportunity were on her side. Her lover came along at a particularly vulnerable period in her life and an affair seemed a sensible option. Often her lover appreciated her at the moment her husband let her down.

Respectable

11. The wife who has an affair is most often a respected woman in her community, with an average sex drive, and she takes her responsibilities as a wife and mother seriously. Often her loyalty to her children is intense. She is well thought of and has many friends, some of whom may be her confidantes and allies.

Considerate

12. Adulterous wives do not necessarily hate their husbands and cheat to get back at them. They may feel short-changed, but they

often consider their husbands decent providers and good fathers, so they are careful not to hurt them. A few, like men, simply want more adventure.

Resourceful
13. Wives with lovers learn to be fast thinking, self-reliant, and resourceful, in order to carry off the affair.

Practical
14. Wives with lovers are not usually romantic dreamers or fools. They are pragmatic, even opportunistic when necessary. They recognize the limitations of their affair and do not view their lover as Prince Charming.

Take Risks
15. Wives who enter an extramarital affair are willing to take the chance they may be caught. Stolen moments with a lover are worth all the trouble. They live for those moments.

Reasonable
16. Women who take lovers are not usually swept off their feet by the heat of grand passion. They enter the relationship cautiously, although they may fall in love, and they try to lead with their heads as well as their hearts.

Familiarity
17. They often choose for their lover a man with whom they are already friendly. Not a stranger, but someone familiar, someone for whom they already feel bonds of friendship or admiration. Often they create acceptable social situations where they can meet their lover and even see him when with their respective families.

"Forbidden Fruit"
18. The risk involved in the affair is an added turn-on. It heightens their excitement and pleasure to be doing something "wrong," something off-limits. Secret sin is more delicious than the marriage bed.

Sex and Love
19. Trouble with their spouse began at the feeling level: perhaps some insult, insensitivity, or rejection. They are hungry to give and

receive love. Good sex is dependent on the good feeling they share with their lover.

Emotional Involvement

20. They become emotionally involved with their lovers. The "zipless fuck" is not for them, and their affairs are not based on pure sex. Often their lovers become their best friends. They care about each other's lives; they talk about their jobs, children, and problems. They often call their lovers their real husbands.

❋   ❋   ❋

There is one especially startling finding that arises out of these interviews with married women: They feel entitled to their love affairs. They are beginning to assume the same unsaid rights that men have long assumed. They may be moved toward an affair out of desperation, boredom, or longing, or simply out of a desire for adventure and variety—but in each case they express their sense of entitlement. "I deserved it," they say.

These women speak of fidelity, not only to husbands, children, and the family, but to themselves.

"Your first loyalty is to yourself," said a 30-year-old college professor. For one woman that may mean taking a lover. For another it signifies monogamy. The important point is the focus on the self. "A woman cannot rely on her husband to give her life meaning," Dr. Joyce Brothers warns. "Ultimately, she alone is responsible for her happiness."

The number of married women who take lovers is increasing. With more than half the nation's mothers already working outside the home, women are bound to feel the attentions of other men. Dr. Douglas Sprenkle of the Department of Family Studies at Purdue University now estimates that 40 percent of women have extramarital affairs. And they do not necessarily call themselves "unfaithful."

When there is an abundance of love and respect in marriage, sexual fidelity is no sacrifice. However, sexual infidelity is not the worst betrayal. It is not the only or ultimate act of cheating. In *The Marriage Premise*, Nena O'Neill concludes: 'Sexual fidelity must be kept in perspective; it is not the ultimate virtue, nor does it make a person moral." There are a number of ways to cheat a spouse—financially or emotionally—that have nothing to do with sex. "One

223

can be sexually faithful to a mate and deceive him in a myriad of ways both subtler and vital."*

The passion of romantic love is said to have a usual span of perhaps three years, and in most very good relationships it undergoes a sea change. A marriage that begins with passion and romance may evolve into the permanent bond of two people who no longer thrill to each other's touch as they once did, but who rely on each other's presence and personality much more than mere lovers ever could.

For some men and women, this natural change seems negative and connotes a loss. They yearn for the restoration of romance and passion that an affair provides. Often they separate and divorce. According to the United States Census, 96 percent of the population marries, and of those who divorce, 79 percent remarry.

Despite cracks in the dream, most people hope the spouse they choose will last a lifetime. Marriage is still regarded as the single greatest adventure two people can embark upon together. As society continues to put a premium on the impersonal and the mechanistic, marriage is one bond that offers continuity and intimacy in our lives.

What are the most startling findings that came out of these interviews?

1. As entitlement becomes an important part of women's thinking, more wives will seek pleasure in love affairs. For a woman who has spent her life putting others' pleasure first, taking a lover may be her compromise between responsibility to her family and her personal needs.

2. A wife's love affair, however, is not prima facie evidence that a marriage is nearly over. Nor is it proof that the relationship between husband and wife is dead.

3. More women are feeling capable of balancing a husband and a lover. They can deal with the risks of having an affair. Financially, emotionally, and sexually they feel strong enough to handle it.

*Page 202.

4. While many affairs result from a need not met in the marriage, a growing number of women, like men, say they simply enjoy the adventure and variety. They believe that if the spouse doesn't know, no one is hurt.

5. An affair may no longer be viewed simply as a negative reaction to marriage. It could become the starting point to repair a marriage and reevaluate the long-standing bond of husband and wife.

6. As women move more freely into the work force, friendships and shared interests with men will increase their opportunities for affairs. A working woman may then decide to seize the moment and have an affair.

7. Sex with a lover can turn out to be superior to marital sex. Feeling freer, more experimental, burdened with less domestic responsibility, a woman can experience sexual pleasure not found in her marriage.

8. The new fidelity has raised women's aspirations and rearranged their priorities. While still devoted to family and children, their loyalty to themselves may now allow them to experience love with another man.

9. A wife's affair will continue to be viewed by husbands as the ultimate betrayal. But it may not break up the marriage. As men become more sensitive to women's needs, they may view an affair with less finality.

10. Affairs are and will be viewed with more compassion by the general public. Not approval, but understanding and sympathy.

11. Love affairs may be a search for passion and romance. If she had them once, they may have been lost. She wants to feel alive again.

12. Fear of a husband's finding out about her lover is probably the greatest deterrent a woman faces when contemplating an affair. A woman weighs which she values most: the affair or the marriage. Then she chooses and acts.

13. Boredom, a recurring theme of wandering husbands, is now freely cited by wives who take a lover.

14. A first affair generally begins in the thirties when a women is most vulnerable. It is a time when she is feeling sexually alive, but romance has faded and pressures of building careers and raising children seem burdensome responsibilities. She wants some fun.

15. Taking one's first lover is a traumatic event in a married woman's life. Many women give credit to the "moment." Timing and opportunity make an affair possible.

16. Some married women are able to successfully balance a husband and a lover. They feel genuine affection—however different—for each man.

It is easy to say that an extramarital affair results from a failed marriage, or to lay it at the doorstep of whichever spouse failed to provide the other with support.

But isn't there also something else at work? Something in the quality of our lives that invites infidelity? A climate of boredom, hostility, and depersonalization? A sameness in what we eat, how we dress, and the homes we live in?

We lunch at fast-food chains that dish up preproportioned meals on paper plates; we take coffee breaks standing around vending machines that sell junk food; and we use thousands of disposable, dispensable products every day. We walk nervously down noisy, dirty city streets; we deal with indifferent, careless salespeople; we accept shoddy goods, machines that break down, and cars that are ridden with factory defects. We own more objects: more stereos, more televisions, more calculators. But even the services we receive are less enjoyable. We suffer strikes, slowdowns, and sick-ins that cripple hospitals, transportation, and garbage collection. And we learn to live defensively, fearful of burglaries, muggings, and crime.

Our highways are nearly interchangeable. Are we in Texas or Maine? There are Exxon, Kentucky Fried Chicken, Radio Shack, Sears, MacDonalds in nearly identical shopping malls across the country. More and more products. Less and less quality. What does this do to the quality of our lives?

We live in nuclear famiies far away from grandmas and grandpas who could add the weight of their presence, experience, and traditions. There is little continuity from which to draw, and each family must start anew. Who is there to fall back on or call up when trouble comes? Our days are so crammed with duties to dispatch, responsibilities to perform, and chores to accomplish that we've less and less time to spend together to enjoy the human experiences.

These attitudes overflow into the way we respond to each other. We make instant friends, but often those relationships are short-lived. We move around, changing jobs, careers, and homes. So we may mistake sharing a joint for friendship, or sex for caring.

Given the conditions of these times, extramarital sex can fit in rather comfortably. It can relieve tedium and boredom. It can establish human contact with another person. It can be a safety valve to release job tension, family tension, and sexual tension.

What the majority of wives want is a loving relationship, a continuing love affair, an emotional-sexual bond in which commitment, responsibility and passion are felt for each other. One third of married women are saying that when they didn't find it at home, they sought it elsewhere.

Imperfect marriages will continue to exist. So will love affairs. And more wives will try loving two men. Modern marriage demands that we look at these women and examine their motivations from a new perspective.

A love affair touches so many people—wives, husbands, lovers, children, grandparents, friends. Chances are that almost everybody will encounter this situation at some time. Perhaps you have already faced it, or faced the possibility that it could happen to you.

That's a fact we have to face as a society. And it's a choice each woman must make for herself.

BIBLIOGRAPHY

Barbach, Lonnie Garfield. *For Yourself—The Fulfillment of Female Sexuality*. New York: Doubleday, 1975.

Bartusis, Mary Ann. *Every Other Man: How to Cope with Infidelity and Keep Your Relationship Whole*. New York: Dutton, 1978.

Beauvoir, Simone de. *The Second Sex*. New York: Knopf, 1953.

Brothers, Joyce. *The Brothers System for Liberated Love and Marriage*. New York: Avon, 1973.

_____. *How to Get What You Want Out of Life*. New York: Simon and Schuster, 1978.

Butler, Robert N. and Lewis, Myrna I. *Sex After Sixty: A Guide for Men and Women for Their Later Years*. New York: Harper and Row, 1976.

Caine, Lynn. *Widow*. New York: Bantam, 1975.

Chapman, A. H., M.D. *Marital Brinkmanship*. New York: Putnam, 1974.

Chesler, Phyllis. *Women and Madness*. New York: Doubleday, 1972.

Cohen, Susan. *The Liberated Couple*. New York: Lancer, 1971.

Colette, Sidonia Grabella. *Cheri*. France: Fayard, 1920.

Comfort, Alex. *The Joy of Sex*. New York: Crown, 1972.

Decter, Midge. *The Liberated Woman and Other Americans.* New York: Coward McCann Geoghegan, 1971.

Deming, Barbara. *We Cannot Live Without Our Lives.* New York: Grossman, 1974.

Dowling, Colette. *The Cinderella Complex.* New York; Summit Books, 1981.

Ellis, Albert. *Sex Without Guilt.* Secaucus, N.J.: Lyle Stuart, 1966.

Ellis, Havelock. *Studies in the Psychology of Sex.* New York: Random House, 1936.

Epstein, Joseph. *Divorced in America.* New York: Dutton, 1974.

Ferguson, Mary A., ed. *Images of Women in Literature.* Boston: Houghton Mifflin, 1973.

French, Marilyn. *The Woman's Room.* New York: Summit Books, 1977.

————. *The Bleeding Heart.* New York: Summit Books, 1980.

Friday, Nancy. *My Secret Garden: Women's Sexual Fantasies.* New York: Trident, 1973.

————. *Men in Love.* New York: Delacorte, 1980.

Friedan, Betty. *The Feminine Mystique.* New York: Dell, 1962.

Fromm, Erich. *The Art of Loving.* New York: Harper and Row, 1956.

Gelb, Arthur and Gelb, Barbara. *O'Neill.* New York: Harper and Row, 1974.

Gold, Herbert. *He She.* New York: Arbor House, 1980.

Gornick, Vivian and Moran, Barbara K. eds. *Woman in Sexist Society: Studies in Power and Powerlessness.* New York: Basic, 1971.

Gould, Lois. *Such Good Friends.* New York: Random House, 1970.

Greer, Germaine. *The Female Eunuch.* New York: McGraw Hill, 1971.

Hallberg, Edmond C. *The Gray Itch: The Male Metapause Syndrome.* New York: Stein and Day, 1978.

Hite, Shere, ed. *Sexual Honesty: By Women for Women.* New York: Warner Books, 1974.

————. *The Hite Report.* New York: Dell, 1977.

————. *The Hite Report on Male Sexuality.* New York: Knopf, 1981.

Hunt, Morton. *Sexual Behavior in the Seventies.* New York: Dell, 1975.

Janeway, Elizabeth. *Man's World, Woman's Place: A Study in Social Mythology.* New York: William Morrow, 1971.

_____. *Between Myth and Morning: Women Awakening.* New York: William Morrow, 1974.

Jones, William and Jones, Ruth. *Two Careers–One Marriage.* New York: American Management, 1980.

Jong, Erica. *Fear of Flying.* New York: Holt, 1973

_____. *How to Save Your Own Life.* New York: Holt, 1977.

_____. *Fanny.* New York: New American Library, 1980.

Kassorla, Irene. *Nice Girls Do.* Los Angeles: Stratford Press, 1981.

Kinsey, Alfred C. et al. *Sexual Behavior in the Human Female.* Philadelphia: Saunders, 1953.

_____. *Sexual Behavior in the Human Male.* Philadelphia: Saunders, 1948.

Kuten, Jay. *Coming Together, Coming Apart.* New York: Macmillan, 1974.

Lederer, William J. and Jackson, Don D. *The Mirages of Marriage.* New York: W. W. Norton, 1968.

Le Shan, Eda. *The Wonderful Crisis of Middle Age.* New York: David McKay, 1973.

Lewis, Helen Block. *Psychic War in Men and Women.* New York: NYU Press, 1976.

Masters, William H. et al. *The Pleasure Bond: A New Look at Sexuality and Commitment.* Boston: Little Brown, 1975.

Masters, William H. and Johnson, Virginia E. *Human Sexual Response* Boston: Little Brown, 1966.

_____. *Human Sexual Inadequacy.* Boston: Little Brown, 1970.

May, Rollo, *Love and Will.* New York: W. W. Norton, 1969.

Mayer, Nancy. *The Male Mid-Life Crisis: Fresh Starts After Forty.* New York: Doubleday, 1978.

McCarthy, Mary. *Memoirs of a Catholic Girlhood.* New York: Harcourt Brace, 1957.

Miller, Jean Baker, ed. *Psychoanalysis and Women.* Baltimore: Penguin, 1973.

Millet, Kate. *Flying.* New York: Knopf, 1974.

Murstein, Bernard I. *Love, Sex and Marriage Through the Ages.* New York: Springer Publishing, 1974.

Nin Anaïs. *The Diary of Anaïs Nin.* New York: Harcourt Brace World, 1966.

————. *Delta of Venus: Erotica.* New York: Harcourt Brace Jovanovich, 1977.

Oates, Joyce Carol. *Wheel of Love and Other Stories.* New York: Vanguard Press, 1970.

————. *Marriages and Infidelities.* New York: Vanguard Press, 1972.

Olsen, Tillie. *Silences.* New York: Delacorte, 1978.

O'Neill, Nena. *The Marriage Premise.* New York: M. Evans, 1977.

O'Neill, Nena and O'Neill, George. *Open Marriage: A New Life Style for Couples.* New York: M. Evans, 1972.

————. *Shifting Gears.* New York: M. Evans, 1974.

O'Reilly, Jane. *The Girl I Left Behind.* New York: Macmillan, 1980.

Pietropinto, Anthony and Simenauer, Jacqueline. *Beyond the Male Myth: What Women Want to Know about Men's Sexuality, A National Survey.* New York: Time Books, 1977.

Plath, Sylvia. *The Bell Jar.* New York: Harper and Row, 1971.

Ptaschkina, Nelly. *Diary.* Translated by Pauline de Chary. Boston: Small Maynard and Co., 1923.

Reik, Theodore. *A Psychologist Looks at Love.* New York: Rinehart, 1944.

Rodgers, Carl. *Becoming Partners: Marriage and Its Alternatives.* New York: Delacorte, 1972.

Rothman, Sheila M. *Woman's Proper Place: A History of Changing Ideals and Practices, 1870 to the Present.* New York: Basic, 1978.

Roy, Maria, ed. *Battered Women: A Psychological Study of Domestic Violence.* New York: Van Nostrand Reinhold, 1977.

Scarf, Maggie. *Unfinished Business: Pressure Points in the Lives of Women.* New York: Doubleday, 1980.

Schall, Maxine. *Limits: A Search for New Values.* New York: Potter Clarkson, 1981.

Schultz, Terry. *Bittersweet: Surviving and Growing from Loneliness.* New York: Crowell, 1976.

Sheehy, Gail. *Passages: Predictable Crises of Adult Life.* New York: Dutton, 1976.

Spock, Benjamin. *The Common Sense Book of Baby and Child Care.* New York: Duell, Sloan and Pearce, 1957.

Szasz, Thomas. *The Manufacture of Madness.* New York: Harper and Row, 1970.

Talese, Gay. *Thy Neighbor's Wife.* New York: Doubleday, 1980.

Tavris, Carol and Sadd, Susan. *The Redbook Report on Female Sexuality.* New York: Dell, 1978.

Tennov, Dorothy. *Love and Limerence: The Experience of Being in Love.* New York: Stein and Day, 1979.

Terkel, Studs. *Working: People Talk about What They Do All Day and How They Feel about What They Do.* New York: Pantheon Books, 1972.

Toffler, Alvin. *Future Shock.* New York: Bantam, 1971.

_____. *The Third Wave.* New York: Morrow, 1980.

Walster, Elaine and Walster, William G. *A New Look at Love.* Reading, Mass: Addison-Wesley, 1978.

West, Uta. *If Love Is the Answer, What Is the Question?* New York: McGraw Hill, 1977.

Wolfe, Linda. *Playing Around: Women and Extramarital Sex.* New York: Morrow, 1975.

Woolf, Virginia. *A Room of One's Own.* New York: Harcourt Brace, 1929.

Yglesias, Helen. *Sweetsir.* New York: Simon and Schuster, 1981.

Ziskin, Jay and Ziskin, Mae. *The Extra-Marital Sex Contract.* Los Angeles: Nash, 1973.

INDEX

Index